THE JUNIOR PHILOSOPHICAL SOCIETY

Tony Thorne MBE

THE JUNIOR PHILOSOPHICAL SOCIETY

First edition September 2001
ISBN 0-905-119-10-4
Second Printing November 2004

Second edition May 2007
ISBN 978-1-4116-9623-5

This is the third edition January 2016
ISBN 9781523748167

This book is dedicated to Livia and Ian – The future is yours now… so try to look after it.

Cover photo by the author.

Published by Etcetera Press & Amazon

Author's Introduction to the 3rd. edition.

What makes some children, as well as their parents, behave as they do nowadays? That was first written back in 1985, but it's even more relevant today. Some of the possible reasons are examined in this study of a group of intelligent children, and the meetings they held to discuss everything about life now and in the future. In many subjects, they soon found they were better informed than many of their elders. When they apply their devastating logic to analyze what they are told, and what they learn elsewhere, their conclusions range from hilarious to the deadly serious. This still happens today, with the Internet available to them, and can even lead to contempt… and relevant behavior.

The Subjects these children explore include Computers, Alien Visitations, Politics, Creation, Human Behavior, The Supernatural, Time Travel, Evolution and Religion. Plus comments on Cosmology, as well as Astrology, and the probable end of the civilized World as we, or rather they know it. Their conclusions often raise more questions than provide answers, but they might also prompt relevant readers to reconsider their attitude towards children, as well as the questions they ask. Especially in the light of the, rapidly accelerating, information revolution surrounding, and even submerging, many of us today.

Things are not as comfortable as they used to be, and will never be again. We cannot any more keep children quiet with patronizing answers. They can now easily find out about all kinds of things, and in ways that earlier generations never could, as this book shows! When the members of the Junior Philosophy Society apply their devastating youthful logic to what they discover, and then compare it with what the older generation tries to tell them, the seeds of distrust already sown, inevitably begin to grow! Finally, when some of their parents begin to suspect what is going on, they too react in ways that reflect how they were brought up!

CONTENTS - in date order

(if you only want to read the minutes)

PUBLISHER's INTRODUCTION FOR GROWNUPS

Why do so many children, as well as some parents, behave in the ways they do nowadays? Could it be due to the rapidly growing communications revolution, multi-channel satellite television, computers and most of all now the Internet?

Prior to television, most individuals, young or old then, had little real contact with what was going on in the big world outside their own very limited environment. Things are different today. We have become directly exposed to global world news and can see it all happening.

TV newscasters routinely tell us that some of the pictures about to be shown may be disturbing to sensitive viewers. Some concerned parents will immediately reach for the On/Off switch. But many of them don't make it in time, or don't care. Often, inevitably, they aren't even there and children watching alone will surely continue to watch. Their intelligence, and perhaps most of all sensitivity, will determine their level of understanding of what follows.

But there are still problems even if the 'Off' option is exercised. Children immediately want to know why. Almost any kind of answer will make them curious. Then, sooner or later, watch something most adults would think they shouldn't, they surely will. They'll probably be alone at the time too. The question is, how old, or even how young, should any sensitive child be, to be safely exposed to what adults can see most nights of the week? Do we really know? Are time and age limits really effective when children are not all the same.

Children learn from what they hear, see, and experience directly. More and more now, they are becoming influenced by the information technology explosion in all its manifestations. When they compare what they learn from it, with what they learn erratically from their parents and dogmatically from some of their teachers, their feelings about society and its behaviour must become more and more confused. The seeds of distrust of society, as well as of their parents and teachers must surely grow in their receptive young minds, and soon become reinforced. Could this be why some of them become withdrawn and insecure, while others become aggressive and contemptuous of any kind of authority?

This book identifies many of the things intelligent children want to know about today. It also explores how they get to know about things, and how they react to the ways adults do, or do not, understand and behave towards them. Children, unlike many adults, do not make up their minds rapidly about things and then only look for that new event, or piece of information, which confirms what they've decided is right, ignoring anything else.

They take everything in and analyze it logically and, as what follows shows, their observations can range from hilarious to deadly serious … and often even controversial.

The book is designed for browsing. It can be dipped into almost anywhere, backwards and forwards, depending upon the reader's interests and personal beliefs.

THE JUNIOR PHILOSOPHICAL SOCIETY - ***My diary and the Minutes. How I got it all started!***

My name is Alan Charles and I'm eleven and three quarters years old. I live in a village near the end of a little town in Southern England. There isn't much for children to do here, but I do have some good friends and we like to meet and discuss things that seem important to us about the world. The things we can't discuss with our parents.

Before we started our society, I used to do things differently. Every night, if it seemed important I wrote things down in my secret diary. Things about what I heard and saw and read about. Everything to do with growing up and understanding about life. Then I got a computer for my birthday last year and started to copy everything into it as well as anything new that turns up. Nowadays, I still do that, and I also keep things ready for our next meeting, or for when we next discuss that special subject. If I can't remember everything that happened I don't worry about it. I decided some time ago that's a good way to sort out the really important things.

I got fed-up trying to write everything in my diary every day, there wasn't enough space. There's more room in an ordinary notebook, but a computer is better. It's so much quicker, and safer from grown-ups wanting to see everything in it. I can switch the screen very fast if anyone comes in to have a look! With my word-processing program, the files can be any size I want to make them. It took me some time to enter what I'd written in the old way in my notebook, even though it was mostly only one entry to put in at the end of each week. Now at last, after a lot of work, I've got everything up-to-date, and I´ve burnt my old diary. Reading through it all now, on the screen, I soon realized that there's so much I don't understand and want to discuss with my friends, so I've worked out how to do it.

I've decided to start a new Club and hold the meetings at home, here upstairs in My Room. My parents say I can, as long as we're not more than five or six members and never noisy, or break anything. And I've promised to make sure we all wipe our shoes properly, on the front doormat when we come in. All my best, most important, friends think it's a really good idea, and I'm going to be the Secretary and put the notes I make, at our meetings, on to my computer.

Alf Brodie is going to be the Chairman because he's nearly twelve and is the oldest. Mike Thomas and Joe Bennett are only nine, so they haven't got any special jobs to do yet. Sylvie Richards is eleven and really quite clever. She says she wants to be Assistant Secretary and help me print out the Notes ... to perhaps make them up into a book one day. We could try to do that at the end of our first year, then each year of meetings after that. It sounds like a good idea.

We're going to call it THE JUNIOR PHILOSOPHY CLUB and will try to have at least one meeting every month, on a Saturday afternoon. Perhaps two or three, or even more during the holidays, especially if it's raining. At our first meeting, which is going to be this Saturday afternoon at 3 p.m. we're going to discuss what subjects we should talk about in the future.

MINUTES OF THE FIRST MEETING OF THE JUNIOR PHILOSOPHICAL SOCIETY on Saturday April 26

Present: Alf Brodie (Chairman)
Alan Charles (Secretary)
Sylvia Richards (Deputy Secretary)
Mike Thomas (Member)
Joseph Bennett (Member)

Subject: Things we want to discuss at our future Meetings.
We looked at some records of Meetings one of our parents had to do with the local Golf Club Committee. We decided we should make our Notes into what are called Minutes of Meetings too, but a lot more interesting.

We also improved the name of our Club. A Society is more like we really want it to be. Sylvie said she thought it sounded more important than to call it just a Club.

After that, we all talked about the all subjects which interest us and agreed on these to have first, but not necessarily in this order: -

EVOLUTION including dinosaurs.
TIME TRAVEL to the past and future.
RELIGION including Heaven and Hell, and anything else to do with it like Angels and Cherubs.
THE UNIVERSE and how it started.
SPACE TRAVEL.
THE SUPERNATURAL including Miracles.
ALIENS and UFOs.
COMPUTERS including Robots.
THE FUTURE, right up to the end of it, whenever that is.
POLITICS ...?

Mike and Joe didn't want Politics, and Sylvie wasn't very interested. Alf and Alan said it was an important subject that would affect our future when we become grown-ups. Our parents seem to talk about it a lot. All the newspapers and TV seem to be full of it, so perhaps it will become interesting to us one day too. Anyway, we agreed we could always start discussing it at a meeting and then change to something more interesting, if it turns out to be really boring, like it seems it would be to some of us now! We also agreed that after each meeting, one of us should find out something important about the subject for the next meeting after that, and then tell us about it to start off the next meeting. I said there were all kinds of things in my diary that I could use.

Alf wanted to be the first to choose a subject, as the Chairman, and said he would like us to discuss EVOLUTION to start things off. I was very glad to agree and second this proposal, which is what they do at the Golf Club Meetings, but we're not going to bother with any more of that fussy stuff. I think it's called protocol, or perhaps it is ritual? Anyway, everybody present finally accepted this as our first subject.

Mike and Joe really wanted ALIENS and UFOs first, and said the Minutes should say that they did. That's why I've put that in. Alf said if we have that subject later, Mike and Joe can introduce it. So they will have even longer to find out as much as they can about it!

Any other business: Going by the Golf Club Minutes, it seems this always goes at the end of a proper meeting. Even when there isn't anything else you should say there isn't. This time though there was something extra from Sylvie. She asked if we should have any Membership Fees, like they do in the Golf Club. She said she could be the Treasurer and look after the money, if we did. Everyone else said no, not really, well not yet anyway, but she could probably have the job if we did, if ever we did.

We didn't discuss anything important after that, except to agree again that EVOLUTION would be the subject of the next meeting, which is going to be next Saturday at 3 pm again.

Back to my diary again.

When I was six years old, or perhaps it was seven, and old enough to start thinking about things, and asking all sorts of questions, I soon had some problems. Everybody grown up only wanted me to listen. They didn't like me asking them any serious questions. I read it somewhere that parents get worried if their children don't begin to talk soon enough! It seems to me that as soon as we do talk, and begin to ask questions, grown-ups always seem to want us to stop!

Well, I listened carefully to what everyone told me. I've always been very curious about things. Everything I hear and learn about more and more makes me want to ask all kinds of questions. But I soon found out that adults really hate this. They usually try anything not to answer me. The trouble is, I usually have even more questions when they do answer me!

Well, some time ago, I got tired of just asking about everything. I decided to write down what I found out as I went along. It's been very useful and very interesting. Every time now, when I look over what I wrote in my old notebooks, I can really tell I'm changing as I get older and learn more about life. I can see too how grown-ups say different things at different times, even about the same things. It must be because they keep changing their mind about things, or perhaps they weren't thinking properly the first time. Sometimes perhaps not even the second time, or even more often than that. Perhaps never with some of them.

Well, that's enough about that. Now I'm coming to all the different subjects I've been thinking about, since I was younger. There are so many of them, but RELIGION is perhaps the hardest of all the subjects to understand. I still find it all very confusing. What I find the hardest to understand is a lot of the things to do with what's called FAITH. This word often seems to have the same meaning as RELIGION to grown-ups, but not always.

It's a lot to do as well with how to get on with other people ... and good behaviour too. Try to be on your best behaviour, my parents are always telling me. Don't go on and on asking embarrassing questions, when we go anywhere. They often say their parents told them that children should be seen and not heard, and how they wish it was still like that today. Especially if ever we go to a church, for any reason, like for a wedding or a funeral of somebody, and I start asking questions about anything I think is really serious.

When I was very little, I soon found out that I mustn't do or say anything about the things that I found the most interesting. Anything they didn't mind me doing or saying usually turned out to be rather boring. I think they'd had enough of me bothering them all the week. I think that was why, by Sunday afternoon, I had to go to a Sunday School. It was a funny sort of school really. The classroom in the church hall was very small. There was only one teacher and not many children like at normal school. The lessons seemed a bit boring at first, but after a bit, because there was nothing else to do, I had to listen and then I began to get more interested. It was all about what you're supposed to believe in. It made me think about things quite a lot.

I soon found out that grown-ups seem to need to believe in all kinds of things, even though they may not always seem to be really true and able to have happened. I remember the first time I asked my parents where I came from. They said I wasn't old enough to ask questions like that, even though I was already doing it.

My grandmother didn't say that though, when I decided to ask her. She said God made me, as well as all the other children I knew. All the children in the world, everywhere. This was quite interesting, but hard to believe. I knew there were a lot of people alive in the world, because I've seen lots of them on TV. There are ever so many in the towns and cities everywhere and in all the different countries. There seems to be millions and millions of them, all living their own lives, wherever they are. It must have been a lot of work making all of them, I remember thinking at the time. I remember wondering too where he, I mean He, did it, and why so many, and what they were all made from.

Nowadays, thanks to all my books and disks and the older boys at school, and some of the new lessons we've having lately, I do know where they all come from. It's really nothing like what I used to be told at all. God doesn't seem to have anything to do with it, as far as I can see, only our parents and doctors and nurses.

Grown-ups often say things that aren't true. Look at that story they used to tell me about Father Christmas bringing all my presents. I never could see why I had to thank my parents and all my relatives for presents, if he brought them. When they explained that Santa Claus (or sometimes they called him Father Christmas), only delivered everything, I used to think he had enough work just bringing all the toys without having to go around collecting them from all the different relatives in the first place. Especially the presents I got from my own parents, which I often used to discover hidden up on a shelf. Why couldn't they deliver them?

It wasn't long before I found out he wasn't a real person at all, just somebody made up. Grown-ups are really strange about these pretending kind of things. I suppose it makes them happy, to see little children believing in funny things like that.

MINUTES OF THE FIFTH MEETING OF THE JUNIOR PHILOSOPHICAL SOCIETY on Saturday July 26th.

Present: Alf Brodie (Chairman)
Alan Charles (Secretary)
Sylvia Richards (Deputy Secretary)
Mike Thomas (Member)
Joseph Bennett (Member)
Fred Clarke (Member)

Minutes of the last Meeting: When I reminded everybody, that the last meeting was all about the Supernatural and Telepathy and Telekinesis, nobody wanted me to read them out. So I didn't.

Subject: HUMAN BEHAVIOUR

What sort of a subject is that, Mike wanted to know. We never had it in our list when we started these meetings?

Alf said it was a very important subject for him and he wanted us all to talk about it. He had been in terrible trouble yesterday, with his parents about something and he wanted to talk to us about it. He said that if we got fed up after a bit, he would agree we could go on with anything else we'd rather have. We all agreed this was fair and wanted to help him feel better anyway.

He told us that he'd spent half of his pocket money this week on a special book and his mother had found it in his room. She had got very cross and told his father about it when he came home from work.

What kind of book was it then, Sylvie wanted to know. All pictures of big topless girls I suppose. Why do boys like that sort of silly thing?

No it wasn't, Alf shouted. It was a good magazine about photography. I wanted it to help me with the camera I got for my birthday. How was

I to know it had a section in it like that. It was only two pages, and one of the girls was nearly dressed anyway. Trust my mother to go and pick it up and just open it at the wrong page.

There were pages and pages of pictures of other things, like old men on seats in the park. But mostly flowers and birds and all kinds of things I'm interested in. There were lots of pages about how you set the camera when it isn't sunny.

Anyway, she took it and gave it to my father to throw away. Well he didn't, because he forgot to lock his shed this morning, and I saw it in there. It was opened at the same place my mother found, under a newspaper.

Sylvie asked, What's all that got to do with Human Behaviour then?

Quite a lot surely, Alf said. Why are so many things all right for grownups but not us? They watch films and things on TV, which they say we can't until we're older. But it doesn't happen even then. My big brother is certainly old enough now, but they don't ever seem to watch any films with him when he's home. He always goes over to his friend's house to watch them with him. But only when his friend's parents are out for the evening. So, I think it's not that they don't want us to watch the films. It's them. They don't want to watch late night films with us there to see everything with them.

I said, That's right. It's because they get what's called embarrassed. They get very uncomfortable if the film has anything about sex in it. The trouble is, nowadays it seems to me that every film in the evening has got that in it. Even the adverts. After 9 o'clock you can see and hear all kinds of things grown-ups say we shouldn't.

Alf said, I'm old enough to stay up until 9.30 now and things are getting very strange. My dad always wants to go over to the BBC news at 9 o'clock when I'm watching. Then he gets fed up because he sees some film started at 9 o'clock on one of the different channels we can get. One night last week, he had to go to the telephone and left the TV on one of the satellite film channels. My mother was in the kitchen so I watched about 5 minutes of what looked at first like it was going to be just a boring film about politics. Then they started taking their clothes off in the bedroom, just as my dad finished on the telephone. We don't want to see that rubbish, he said, and switched it off. I went to bed after that. Then I actually heard him switch it on again. I knew it was the same film because the music was exactly the same again, just like when they were in the bedroom.

Joe said, You can always tell by some of the other noises too.

I've got my own video recorder now, Mike said. I often record late night films. I can watch them when my parents are out. A lot of them are boring, but they do have some good monster films on some nights. The trouble is there are so many of them. I want to save them and I never have enough pocket money to keep on buying blank videos.

You can get them very cheap at car-boot sales, I said, Often with something interesting already on them. I found a good one last Sunday, all about Count Dracula. It was quite good, even though it was only in black and white.

Couldn't we see some of your videos at our meetings, asked Fred.

No, I said, It's too dangerous in the daytime. My parents are usually downstairs and could come in any minute and see what we're watching. I don't want to embarrass them.

I know something else strange about grown-ups, Sylvie said. They say it's wrong to talk bad about other people, but they do it all the time. The lady next door is always telling my mother how terrible her other neighbor is. Then they both talk about the big fat lady over the road, who has a horrible barking dog.

I remember I got told off once, when I was very little, I said. I told our next door lady that my dad said she had a big fat bottom. She was bending over at the time, getting a sheet out from a basket to hang on her clothesline. I could see that my dad was right.

Was she very angry then, asked Alf.

Yes, very, I said. She came to our front door and told my dad off. He was really mad at me. Just for telling the truth, but I can see why they both were angry, now that I'm older.

So could everybody else.

Alf said that kind of situation was all about what's called diplomacy. You must be careful what you say to grown-ups and not always tell the truth, even though grown-ups say you must always be honest. But they aren't! We all know they aren't always honest with us, or even with each other, especially each other.

But if they find out you haven't told the truth, they get angry, Sylvie said.

Then you have to be clever enough not to be found out, said Mike. It's something you have to learn in life, as you grow up.

Alf said, It's all about the Laws and Rules of Behavior. You have to have laws about what you can do and what you can't. If we were all good and perfect we wouldn't do anything wrong, so we wouldn't need any laws to break at all. The trouble is, bad people don't take any notice of them anyway, and good people don't really need them do they? It makes you wonder why we even bother to have them.

Sylvie said, That's easy, it's so good people can know what to do with bad people who do wrong things. The laws say what you have to do to people if they break one of them. Like how many days they must go to prison if they rob or kill somebody. Or how much extra money they have to pay, if they don't pay it in the first place, when they should.

I read it somewhere, Fred said, That there's one law you can break which they can't do anything to you when they find out you broke it.

Alf said, Yes, I know that one, it's the law that says you mustn't try to kill yourself. If you do, then that's it! Anyway, he said, I know another crime where they can't do anything to you if you succeed. Guess what it is then?

Nobody could guess the answer, so Alf said, It's starting a revolution to take over the government.

We all thought about that, and decided Alf was right.

I said, I think I know another name for this subject. It's called Morality. That means all about the right way to behave in life. What you should do or should not do. Like never breaking any laws, on purpose anyway.

Like the Ten Commandments in the Bible, said Mike.

Yes, I said, But all the ones the politicians in the government make too, and the ones we have at school. But morality also means behaving nice to other people, doing all the right things. It´s more than just not breaking laws.

Like not throwing stones at cats, said Joe. I don't think there's a law about that, is there? Nobody knew for sure.

Sylvie suddenly said, It's against the law to marry more than one person. But my cousin Jenny has lived with about three different men since she was eighteen. She's twenty-five now. She's all by herself at the moment, but is already thinking about the next one, she told me last week. She only lives with one at a time, but I don't think there's a law against more than one at a time, is there?

None of us had heard of one.

Fred said, I suppose it must be the same if a man lives with more than one girl at the same time. That's interesting, I bet some men are already doing it. Perhaps even in the same house?

So it's against the law if you're married, but O.K. if you're not, said Mike.

Alf said, When you get married, you promise not to ever have anyone else, not ever. That doesn't seem to happen very often though does it? Lots and lots of people get divorced nowadays.

When that happens, Mike said, The man has to pay lots of money to the wife. So it doesn't seem to be a good idea for a man to ever get married then does it? Perhaps that's why lots of them don't nowadays.

Fred said, Getting married must be right if you meet the right person and really love them forever and ever.

Sylvie said, But how can you ever know that. Look at all the millions of people there are in the world. The first nice one to come along might seem to be right for you. Then you would probably get married. Especially if nobody else came along before you did. Then perhaps someone better would come along another day and then you'd fall in love again and want to get divorced.

I said, The idea of getting married is supposed to be to stay with one person and have some children. Then bring them up so that they will marry someone and have children themselves. It's all been evolved to keep the world going. I think it's called having a stable family life.

Sylvie said, Lots of people today have babies without being married, just like the animals do. Do you think that's wrong?

I said, Well, it could be if they don't stay together, and then both find someone else and have some more children. If too many people did that, the world would end up with too many children. Who would look after them all and give them their pocket money every week?

Mike said, My mum and my dad now aren't married. My mum was married to my real dad before, but he didn't like me. I heard him tell my mum one evening that he never wanted me, and when I came it upset their relationship. Then one day he just left and we've never seen him again. Anyway, I like my new dad much better. He plays lots of games with me, and gives me extra pocket money sometimes.

Sylvie said, Do you think he will marry your mother one day?

Mike thought about that, then he said he wasn't sure but he hoped it would happen. Perhaps if she had any more children, he said. But I don't know if I'd really like that. It would be nice to have a little brother, but it might make my new dad think about leaving too. Or perhaps he would like him more than me. I think a little sister might be better.

We all agreed Mike should try to be as good as possible at home, so his new dad would always want to stay.

Finally, to close the meeting, Alf said he was glad to have talked things over with us, and felt better now. Then he said, I'd like us to have this subject again, if everybody will agree to it. Perhaps to talk more about the way grownups think and behave. It seems different between men and women too. My big brother has gone out with lots of different girls. He told me once that sometimes, he can't understand the way they think. He says they use creative logic.

What's that, we all asked, especially Sylvie, who didn't sound very pleased.

Alf said he wasn't sure, but he'd try to find out more about it from his brother ready for when we have this subject again.

Mike suddenly said, I've remembered something I wanted to discuss. I was reading that to kill bacteria in hospitals, all the bedclothes and things have to be steamed at 150 degrees. Yet my mother washes our clothes and things at only 60 degrees and sometimes only 30 degrees. That must mean the bacteria in them don't get killed. Perhaps it's why more and more children and grownups seem to get ill nowadays. My mother has bad asthma, but her mother never had it.

This was something new to the rest of us and it seemed Mike must be right. But we all agreed it was the kind of thing that would make our parents angry if we tried to tell them about it.

Joe made us all laugh pretending to be some bacteria trying to hang on tight in a washing machine. He was really pleased when we all joined in.

Any other business: Sylvie said she was sorry she couldn't come to the next meeting, and not just because it was going to be about Politics. Her two cousins were coming for the weekend and she had to be home with them. No, she didn't think they would want to come. They were too young.

My diary again ... at Sunday School, when I used to go, the teacher told us God was Almighty and he, I mean He, could do no wrong. She said, Yes he did make us and of course He certainly was perfect but we weren't. We were all Sinners. This, as far as I could tell, meant that we were all bad and wicked and had to be saved. But not until after we're dead, she said when I asked. Then I tried to ask her, why did we have to be made so bad in the first place if God was so perfect at doing everything, but she wouldn't answer.

Well, I often do try hard to be good, but I knew even then that I wasn't perfect in mind and body. For one thing, I have a very short neck and have problems with some of my pullovers. Also, I'm good at sums and things, but not History. Anyway, I know a few boys at school who are certainly not perfect and definitely not good, and two at least who are really horrible, especially in the playground.

So the next Sunday, I asked her again what seemed to me a simple question. All I wanted to know was, why didn't God make us all perfect and good too, and not sinners. Especially if He's perfect and we are all created in his image, like she often said. Well, I didn't get any kind of useful answer at all, even though to me it still seems a sensible question. Think of all the arguments, fighting and wars it would save.

Perhaps it would be very boring though, if we were all the same, and only good. Anyway, when I asked next what it was we would be saved from, she told us a bit about Hell and what's called Eternal Damnation. I decided that must be why nobody was ever made perfect. If nobody had to go to those places, then all the work making them would be wasted.

The teacher often used to say that God made man in his image, even though we all look different. When I asked her once if woman was made in His image too, she got a bit confused. She was a big lady and I think she could tell what parts of her I was looking at when I asked that question. I talked about it to my friend Alf. We decided that God must have lots of different images, because it was clear to us that people are all different, in all the different parts of the world, and even here in England, especially all the girls and grown up ladies.

Some other things she told us were interesting though, especially the bits about in the beginning. She said Adam was created as a grownup already. Eve was created from a small part of him. Boys and girls didn't come until later. I nearly asked what nationality Adam and Eve were, and if they'd never been to school, how did they know anything? That would certainly have been another big mistake. It's all quite different from what my science books and computer programs say. They all tell me about Evolution and how life started in the sea, millions and millions of years ago, before human beings ever appeared.

Anyway, the next time I heard that bit about us being made in His image, I had some more questions. I wanted to know if our primitive ancestors, like all the Stone Age people I'd been reading about, as well as bad people, like dictators and serial killers, were all made in his image as well? This really was a mistake. Especially when I said, perhaps it was the quality of the work in making them being not so good, that was the problem with them. I'd heard my dad say that about those new houses over the road near us. There's a lot about them that isn't perfect. Things are always going wrong in them, and my dad says it's the builder's fault, and the cheap materials and parts he used.

Sundays after that, the teacher just talked like I wasn't there. She wouldn't even look at me, or even seem to hear my questions.

I got really fed up with that. In the end I told my mother I wanted to leave, and how about if I joined the Church Choir instead. She seemed very pleased at the idea, but it may have been because I would be out of the way more on Sundays. One night of the week as well, for singing practice. Anyway, I was interested in the idea of being able to talk with older boys about things, and you got paid too! Not a lot, but it was always very useful when my pocket money ran out on Saturdays. I wouldn't really say my voice was special or anything, but it was good enough to pass the test they gave.

We used to have a lot of fun in the Choir. The older boys taught me how to join in and sing different words to some of the hymns, to see if the vicar noticed. He never did, as far as we could tell, nor did anyone else, not even God or any angels. Some of the words were new to me. My parents got angry again when I asked what some of them meant. Anyway, thanks to TV now, and some of the older boys at school, I think I know what most of them mean. Up until then my mother had often said how nice I looked dressed in the special Choir clothes. Cherubic, she said. I had to look that up in my old encyclopaedia. I wasn't very pleased when I found out that I was being called a baby angel.

It did start me thinking again though. Surely there must be mother and father angels? Yet in all the pictures and statues I've ever seen of angels, they all seem to be men. Even the baby ones all seem to be boys. I've never seen any teenager angel pictures or statues either. I wondered why not; if the cherubs grew up to become grown up angels. Where do they come from, and do they keep on coming like we do? Once more nobody wanted to know, or give me any answers. So perhaps cherubs don't grow up and never become big enough to be proper angels and have those shiny rings over their heads. Those halo things you always see in the pictures of angels and saints. I tried asking about what were they for and what were they made from and how did they stay up and not fall off.

Alf Brodie, my best friend, got me into trouble, from laughing, when he said he bet they didn't ever wear a hat over one. Perhaps you could wear a top hat, like the men at the horse racing I saw on television once. I wonder what decides how high up the halo will be over your head and what happens in the night, or if a doorway isn't high enough.

Then there's this thing about angels having wings. That just doesn't seem to be right. Everyone knows birds have wings instead of arms. They don't weigh very much and their arm muscles are strong enough to work the wings. Birds can fly because they don't weigh as much as we do, except for ostriches who nearly do, and can't. So if angels have wings as well as arms, and that's how it looks in all the pictures I've seen, then they must have evolved from something quite different, but what?

Something seems really wrong to me somewhere. Only insects have wings as well as arms and legs. Everything else seems to have wings instead of arms. Anyway, you can only use wings in an atmosphere, like we have here. Perhaps it's like that Santa Claus story again. He certainly couldn't fly around with reindeer pulling his sledge, loaded with presents for every child in the world. Not that they all get anything anyway.

If Heaven is out in space then there's no air there to breathe and make wings work. Also, everyone knows you can't make sounds without air to breathe and talk in, so it seems to me that either Heaven must be very quiet or perhaps they only use thought reading. If not, then I think Heaven would have to be on some other planet where there is air, like here. I wonder where that could be, and how far away it is. It would have to be very big to have enough space for all the people who were good enough to go there. Think how many people have died since the world began. And they go on and on doing it. How could anywhere ever be big enough in the end? Perhaps it depends when the end is. I think its called Judgment Day. I think it'll need a lot more than a day already!

I've really thought a lot about Heaven. Even if not many people are good enough to go there, it must be getting very crowded already. There must be lots of babies there too. Children who die when they are little haven't had time to be bad, or especially wicked. Heaven must have more babies than people by now. I wonder if they still keep growing and who looks after them and feeds them and everybody else. It wouldn't be fair if they never could grow up and enjoy eternity more.

I wonder if old people get younger when they go to Heaven? Especially all the poor old people who can't walk any more. If you die from being ill or hurt in an accident, I suppose you must get better when you get to Heaven. I expect people who can't see, get their eyes back. If not, then Heaven would be full of mostly damaged people, as well as babies! That can't be true. Then there's the problems of Siamese twins, we often see them on TV; do the ones that die get separated in Heaven.

If they still have meals there, I wonder where they get all the food and who does all the washing up? I talked about that with Alf Brodie. He made a joke about perhaps they send all the dirty dishes and things down to Hell for all the bad people to clean. That would be a horrible lot of washing up to do every mealtime, but how could they have water to wash up down there, if it's all very hot? Perhaps they just don't need to eat or drink anything in Heaven?

I wonder what they do all day, if they have days. Perhaps they don't have bodies at all, like when you're alive. But if we're made in God's image and He's there with his body then, at least, we'd need our eyes to be able to see him. I think they must have bodies in Heaven, to be able to enjoy it there, just like you'd need one in Hell, so you didn't enjoy it!

I wonder if they have to go to bed to sleep when it gets dark? Perhaps it never does get dark? If not then I wonder where all the light comes from. Perhaps it comes from all those halo things.

When you're dead, it's for eternity too, which means forever and ever, and that is really a very, very long time. I wonder what do they do all the time to keep interested in things? I think you could do just about everything there is to do in only a thousand years ... and eternity is a lot more than that! I think it could get a bit boring if it just goes on and on and on ..!

I wonder if they really go to sleep in Heaven? It would have to have days and nights there if they do, so it would have to be on some planet with a sun to make days and nights. But with all the people that die every day on this planet, they'd soon run out of room …

unless perhaps Heaven is in more than one place? Perhaps it gets better depending on how good you were before you were dead.

I wonder if you can really meet all your old relatives there as well as all the interesting people already dead? There must be millions of good people from other countries there too. I wonder what language they use in Heaven? There must be more foreign people there than those speaking just English. I often wonder if intelligent aliens go to Heaven too? The universe is so enormous; there must be more of them in it than us. I think they must have their own Heavens. It would take too long for them to get to ours. But perhaps they can if they have faster-than-light space travel there? I wonder if they do?

As to Hell, well by now it must be very, very crowded indeed. I read in a book that more than a thousand babies are born every second on our planet. And the population is growing larger and larger all the time. That means there must be a horrible lot of bad people dying every day, as well as all the good ones. It seems clear to me that Hell can't be down inside our planet. It's all solid at first, then like a very hot liquid metal down to the middle. It's impossible for anyone or anything to be there, if you still have a body. If you don't, then how could you feel all the pain you're supposed to get? Anyway, it can't possibly be so big there for all the space that must be needed. It's really difficult to believe in Hell, unless it's on a big hot planet somewhere. There are plenty of those about as far as I can tell from reading all the books and programs and things I have about astronomy.

Scientists, and space probes, have found out that the ground on Venus is hotter than melted metal, so perhaps the really wicked people are all there jumping up and down on it, all day and night, trying to stop their feet from burning up. They should have a lot of space for them there because it must be all land, and Venus is about the same size as our planet. Perhaps that's where they all are? But if more and more bad people keep getting born and dying it must sooner or later get too crowded. That's the problem with eternity, it keeps on going on and on. Even after what's called Judgment Day, I don't see how it can ever stop, because then it wouldn't be eternity. Time must keep going on and on … whatever.

There seems to be hundreds of things about faith and religion that are not clear to me. It's an enormously important subject. Yet, from the way grown-ups live and talk and go on about everything else, like politics and what's wrong with the government, they don't seem to worry about these things, in faith or religion, that they can't explain to me or even want to talk about. Perhaps understanding about everything comes to you when you get old enough. I hope it does.

MINUTES OF THE SIXTH MEETING OF THE JUNIOR PHILOSOPHICAL SOCIETY on Saturday 20th. September

Present: Alf Brodie (Chairman)
Alan Charles (Secretary)
Mike Thomas (Member)
Joseph Bennett (Member)
Fred Clarke (Member)

Minutes of the last Meeting: We didn't have one last month, because we were mostly all away on holiday with our parents. So the last meeting was the one we had in July. This time I did read out the Minutes.

Nobody wanted anything changed.

Subject: POLITICS

Why do we have to have this subject, Joe wanted to know. It's sure to be very boring. It's the most boring thing you can have on TV. I really think we should change it for something more interesting.

You remember what we said when we started these meeting, Alf said. If it gets boring we'll change to something else.

Anyway, I said, Most grown-ups I know seem to think it's very interesting. They're always going on about the government and what it's doing is always wrong.

Joe said, Anything grown-ups like is usually boring to us. I'd rather have The Future as the subject today.

Alf said, Look, we're having that another time, and anyway, politics is just as much about the future as it is about today. The government has to think about what's going to happen that's not very good for the country, and then decide what to do to stop it happening.

Mike said he thought the politics of a party was like religion. The one you support depends on what you learn from what your parents believe in.

Joe said, That sounds like football too, and what team you support.

I said, Perhaps that means if you are in party politics you are supposed to believe in what the ministers of the government say is best for you and the country, even if they aren't doing it yet.

Alf said, My dad says some of them do try at first, to do what they promise before an election. The trouble is things happen to stop them, then they end up doing the same as any other party.

What sort of things, Joe wanted to know.

Mike said, They have something called a scandal. One of them does something wrong, then the ones not in the government say he must resign from his his job. Usually all the newspapers say the same thing and you get pictures on TV of the different politicians looking cross.

Mike said, Yes, and on all the time too. I think most of it is on after 9 pm. It's all very boring. All the party messages and discussions about them they have. I can't believe I'll ever be interested in listening to them when I'm grown up.

Perhaps why we're not supposed to watch them after 9 o'clock is because of all the bad words they might say about each other, said Fred.

Alf and I agreed. Like the ones we learn from TV films and things.

Mike said he'd never watched a political programme long enough to hear any bad words. But he did switch one on by accident once in the middle of a big discussion round a big table. They were all shouting at each other, one big lady especially was getting very unhappy and noisy. Come to think of it, she did use one word which sounded bad. It made the chief one very cross. It sounded something like - showvinist.

We made him say it again, but nobody at the meeting knew that word. We agreed it must be bad. I certainly couldn't find it anywhere in my computer thesaurus or dictionary, even though most of the bad words we know are in it.

Alf said, Politics is a lot like religion. There really must only be one religion that's really true, but everybody with a different one is sure his is the only one. So, perhaps there's only one party policy that's really the best for people.

I said, Yes, but what's best for rich people is not always what's best for poor people. Perhaps too, what's good for somebody today might not be so good for them tomorrow. Politics is all about knowing what's going to happen next in the future, so you can do something about it, before something happens to stop you doing it.

Say that last bit again, said Alf, so I did, very carefully.

Mike said, My dad says it's unforeseen events that stop politicians doing what they promise to do before they get elected.

Joe wanted to know what an unforeseen event was.

Alf said, It's something serious or important that happens. An event for us can be anything from a birthday party to a big festival. But it's things like a war or something serious happening in another country, or one of those big scandal things, that gives governments a problem they didn't know was coming.

Like the value of our money going up or down suddenly, I said. If our money goes up and all the other countries' money doesn't, then anything we want to sell to another country is more expensive, so they won't buy it. Or perhaps not so much of it as they did before.

Say that again please, said Joe, so I did. Slowly.

Then Joe said, but why would it change? If I have 50p pocket money left, it would always be 50p. How could it change to anything else?

Alf said, it doesn't change, only how much foreign money you can get for it is what changes.

Joe still wanted to know why that would change.

I said, it's all about what's called International Finance. If foreign people start to buy our money, then the price of it goes up. Or if they all start to sell it, then the price goes down. It's changing all the time. If it goes up too much, then the people here, who make things to sell, can't sell them to other countries. Or not so much of it as they did before.

Alf said, They could if they made their prices lower, then they'd sell more to us here too. They must still want to sell things, or some workers would lose their jobs because the companies wouldn't make enough money to pay them.

Joe said, I still don't get it, our money going up and down like that. I think my 50p must still be 50p to me, whatever happens. That's what it is, 50p! Look, I've still got one left here from my pocket money.

That's right, Alf said. But if it did go down and then you wanted to buy something with it from another country, it would cost you more than before. Don't you see?

Joe thought about it for a bit, then he said, But that sounds like it's because the money in another country has gone up. My 50p is still the same, it must be.

We all thought about that.

Then I said, let's get back to Politics. Perhaps we'll understand about International Finance better when we're a bit older.

Alf said, The kind of event that really worries the government is when one of their members dies or does something wrong and has a scandal, so he has to resign. I think this often happens, going by the newspapers. Each time they have to have more little elections for new Members of Parliament. Then they lose them because the people don't like what's going on, and don't vote for them. If they keep on losing them, it could happen one day they don't have enough votes to make new laws or do anything they promised to do and still haven't done yet. That's what really worries them, especially when it's time to have the next big election.

Joe wanted to know what a scandal was.

I said, It's like when the newspapers find out one of them has a secret girl friend somewhere, that his wife doesn't know about. Or even if she does. All the newspapers make a terrible fuss about it, because politicians are supposed to be good and honest and not make mistakes, so that the newspapers find out about them and then make a big fuss.

We all thought about that.

Then Alf said, my dad says politics is like a lot of people in a rowing boat, without a rudder. He said they float on a sea of events with some of them rowing on the left side, and some on the right side. When there's a lot more of them on one side than the other the boat goes round and round and doesn't get anywhere. All the time, the tide is taking them where it wants to anyway. Not only that, some of them even try to row the other way!

Lots of politicians seem very old, Joe said. That must be why they keep dying. If they don't want that to happen they should have more younger ones.

I said, Perhaps they are young in the beginning, but they stay there until they're old and die, or until they have one of those scandals.

Fred said, I think the best kind of government would be where to become a politician you'd have to take examinations like we do at school. Then the best and cleverest ones would belong to one party and become one government. Even if they didn't all agree about what would be best, when they voted on anything, there would be more chance of what most of them wanted being right.

Say that again, I said, so he did.

I want to know why they're called parties, Joe asked. I always thought a party was where you all had a good time and played all kinds of games with each other.

We all thought about that.

Then Mike said, it sounds the same to me. Our parents pay for everything we have at our parties, and they have to pay Income Tax money to the government party.

We all agreed it could be why they were called parties.

Joe said, I'm getting really bored with this subject. How about changing to something more interesting?

Alf said, It's too late to start another subject now and anyway it's stopped raining, let's go out and have a game of football.

Any other business: We forgot to say Sylvie was sorry she couldn't come.

My diary just reminded me about something I noticed the first time I had to go to church. The grown-ups sang and said all the funny words quite naturally, so being much older than I am, and knowing a lot more, they must have had some kind of extra understanding about everything. Not that all of them were awake all the time though.

Perhaps more understanding will come to me too when I'm older. Except for all that stuff about Father Christmas. And I remember my grandmother telling me about Jack Frost. When I asked my dad about him, he said, He doesn't paint our windows at night anymore now. We've got double-glazing! But you can still see what he does to cobwebs in the garden over night when it's freezing. Really! Nothing like how my books say it happens!

Well, I suppose that's what grown-ups mean when they talk about Faith and believing everything about miracles in the Bible. You have to take everything on trust and not have any doubts about it. I think I read that somewhere. Whether it makes sense or not, you're supposed to believe there's a good reason for everything, even if you can't think of one, or even if there really isn't. Well, if nobody will talk any sense to me about it all, I suppose I'll have to wait until I get old enough too. Then I'll either come to understand everything, or perhaps I'll find out that I don't need to worry about any of it either.

MINUTES OF THE FOURTH MEETING OF THE JUNIOR PHILOSOPHICAL SOCIETY on Saturday June 21st.

Present: Alfred Brodie (Chairman)
Alan Charles (Secretary)
Sylvia Richards [Assistant Secretary]
Mike Thomas (Member)
Joseph Bennett (Member)
Frederick Clarke (Member)

Minutes of the last Meeting: I read them out this time and we all decided they were OK with no changes.

Subject: THE SUPERNATURAL, including miracles.

Alf said, This meeting is going to be all about ghosts and things that happen that aren't normal.

As well as things like telepathy and moving furniture about by just thinking at it, asked Sylvie.

Yes, I said, and that's also called the paranormal. Things that happen and must really be like magic, when it isn't just a trick.

Mike said, Just like that man on TV who bends spoons without touching them. People even telephone in and say one of their spoons got bent too, while he was doing it. That's hard to believe.

Joe said, Perhaps it was already bent and they didn't notice it before.

Mike told us he bent a spoon at home last week, by accident, while he was doing up his old roller skates. I couldn't straighten it properly, he said, So I put it back underneath in the drawer and nobody has noticed it yet. I hope that man comes on again soon so I can take it out of the drawer and show everyone.

Do you really think your dad will believe that man did it, asked Sylvie, Would he really be that silly?

Mike wasn't sure, but in the end we all agreed it would be a good idea to try it and see.

Fred said he didn't believe in magic. He thought it was all just tricks. Perhaps you can't see how it's done, but if it's not a normal thing then it must be a trick.

Sylvie said, But what about miracles like in the Bible? What about that miracle where Jesus turned some bread and fishes into enough for hundreds and hundreds of people? I think it was for a lot more than a thousand.

I said, Yes, I've always wondered about that. Did the fishes grow back again when they were cut in half? How long did it take to happen? I expect they had to cook them, so did they grow bigger and bigger during the cooking? Same with the loaves of bread, every time a piece was broken off one, did it come back whole again like magic?

Mike said, I've read that part in the Bible too, but it doesn't say anything at all about how it actually happened. It's just the same with walking on the water. Was the sea flat at the time or was it rough and windy? How could He possibly walk up and down the waves if it was? Anyway, even if it was flat He must have got his feet wet a bit, my mother makes a terrible fuss if I even walk through a little puddle and get my shoes wet.

Sylvie said she expected the sea was flat and somehow it turned solid, as he walked over it. Perhaps he made it freeze into thick enough ice to walk on. Even if not, if it's written in the Bible we should always try to believe it happened, even if we can't really understand how it could.

I said, That's what religion and faith is all about. If you decide you want to believe in something then you have to accept everything about it, even if it isn't normal and you can't understand how it could possibly happen. I suppose that's how grown-ups do it.

We all thought about that.

What about ghosts then, asked Joe, Do they really exist and haunt old castles and spooky places?

Well, Alf said, There seems to be a lot written about them. Some of it must be true. I saw a program on TV where lots of people said they'd seen all kinds of ghosts. They really seemed to believe it.

It's the same with UFOs, I said. But lots of people, especially scientists, don't believe in them. Anyway, I read a theory once that said old rocks are made from the same stuff that computer chips are made from, or rather the other way round. The idea was that in all the rocks that old buildings are made from, there must be some that have chips in them.

We all know that memory chips in computers are getting smaller and smaller, and still more powerful. They're made from silicon which is in all kinds of rocks. There must be tons and tons of it in the old rocks that castles are built from. So, just by luck there could be some chips in the rocks in the castle walls and the doorways, just made naturally by chance. So if some of them are memory chips, anything that happens near them could be recorded. Then later on, the chips could play back what was recorded. Perhaps the temperature could switch it on and off, or some electricity? In spooky films, people always seem to see ghosts and things at night when it's very dark and there's a thunderstorm on.

I suppose that might explain funny sounds being heard, said Mike, But it's hard to believe it might make a ghost appear and walk about, and the temperature to get all cold like I read happens sometimes.

Perhaps it could if the chips could make the recording into a hologram, Fred said. The energy to make it happen could come from the air and then make it cold.

We all knew about holograms and agreed that might be possible. We'd all seen them in shop windows and on cards and things. Alf and I had seen some fantastic ones in a museum in London when our parents took us there last year. Some of them were moving about in a special glass box, but most of them were fixed.

Going back to bending things, I said, How about trying an experiment? Let's see if we can bend something.

Everyone was interested in this idea, so I got a wire coat hanger from my wardrobe and put it on my worktable. Then I said, Now let's all think at it very hard and try to make it bend. The bending force will be much stronger if all of us do it together. Everyone thought this was a good idea, so we tried it for about ten minutes. But, nothing happened.

Then Mike laughed and said, I'm the strongest, and I was thinking it not to do anything. Joe said he was too. The rest of us were not pleased about that, so we all agreed to be serious and try again. We all waited for quite a few minutes but still nothing happened.

Then Joe showed us a normal looking spoon he'd brought. He said it was one he'd bent that morning and then made it straight again. Nobody believed him, and you couldn't see any hammer marks, or anything on it.

Alf said, Let's try again with Joe's spoon. If he did it before, then we should be able to do it again.

Joe said, No, I'll be in trouble at home if it does get bent and stays like it.

Nobody else thought it would anyway, but he wouldn't let us try, just in case.

Sylvie said, What about telepathy then? Guessing cards you can't see, and all that kind of thing? She'd brought some with her specially for this meeting, so we decided to try it.

I said, there's 52 cards in the pack plus 2 Jokers. So that's only 1 chance in 54 of getting one right from the whole pack each time. I think we can say it is telepathy if anyone gets more than that and keeps on doing it.

We took it in turns to try. Sylvie asked us what the next card would be when she turned it over.

After about half an hour of this, we just gave up. Nobody got anything right at all.

I said, That's very unusual. Altogether we tried more that 75 times and nobody got anything right. I think that could be very important for a scientist to know.

Not if he ever wants to win the Lottery, said Alf.

Perhaps we could try for a longer, I said, It should even up to 1 right every 54 goes in the end. Perhaps it depends on how long you try it.

Alf said, Yes, but perhaps it could take a week. We decided to give up.

Mike said, Let's try moving things by just thinking. Perhaps that's easier to do than bending things.

Yes, I said, That should be much more interesting. I think it's what's called telekinesis. After trying to decide what we could move, I found a little button in my pocket and put it on the table. Then we all sat around it, ready to start thinking.

Joe said, I bet it will be just like bending things and won't work for us either. Well, we tried it and it didn't, so he was right.

We decided this subject was getting to be boring, It was time to stop anyway, so Alf ended the meeting, saying that if anything happens that we can't explain or understand, then that's supernatural. That is, until we can explain it, if ever.

Like nothing ever working for us when we try it, said Joe.

Any other business: Nothing, we were all too fed up to want any, anyway. We decided the next meeting would be on Saturday July 26th.

Diary Notes again

It was when I got a book about dinosaurs that I really began to wonder about creation and everything. Something was really wrong. The book said that our planet is about 4,600 million years old. That is an incredible long time. Even if the scientists are a few hundreds of thousands years wrong about this, it doesn't really matter, because it's a lot more than seven days anyway.

The book had a very good idea. If you divide this very big number of years by 100 million you get just 46 super years to think about, which makes it an easier way of looking at things. Well, it was a big surprise to me, the dinosaurs only started about a year ago looking at it as if our world started only 46 super years ago. So it took 45 of them just to get to the beginning of the dinosaurs! That really did surprise me. It seems we know from all the bones and fossils that dinosaurs existed for over 140 million ordinary years, a long time before human beings came. We've only been here around 3 million years, according to that book. I've read the same thing in a new computer encyclopaedia program I have now, so it must be really true. Anyway, in the 46 super years way of looking at it, we began here only 4 super hours ago. That really is amazing. This way of looking at things seems very important too.

I couldn't help wondering, what was God doing all those millions and millions of years before we started? Or even before the dinosaurs started? Perhaps he was looking after life on some other planet? Or perhaps trying out lots of different kinds of intelligent life forms first, before seeing how we would turn out.

Going back to the dinosaurs, when they were here, it seems they were evolving all that time. I've got a lot more books and things about dinosaurs now. Some of them were very big and fierce. Some drawings show how some of them got smaller and quicker as they developed. Perhaps they even got more and more clever too. I wonder if any of them developed any kind of intelligence in their last few million years out of the 140 million. They had longer than us in which to do it. If they did then perhaps they would even have had religions like we do? If they did become intelligent then perhaps they wondered about who made them? Perhaps they even thought they were made like Him and killed any others who didn't agree with them. Nobody has found any signs of any of that yet as far as I know, but it would be really interesting if they did.

When the bones and things were first discovered, nobody was really sure about how old they were and why they all disappeared. They found more and more bones and fossils and realized there were lots of different ones. Some were very small and some were enormous. All through those 140 million years different ones appeared then died out, all at different times. Newer ones that appeared must have been cleverer or faster and more dangerous and ate up the older and weaker ones. It must have been a terrible time. Then one day, or year, or whatever, they all disappeared.

My books and programs say it was probably due to a giant meteorite, or a comet, which hit the earth and exploded. All the dust from the explosion went up into the clouds all around the planet, so the sun couldn't shine through and keep everything warm enough any more. The big dinosaurs especially couldn't survive that so they all died out. The little mammals that were around then could, because they didn't need so much to eat and I suppose they could dig down deep enough to keep warm. They probably had fur to help too, which I suppose the dinosaurs didn't have. I read that all the birds we have around now are descended from some kinds of little dinosaurs that survived whatever killed off all the bigger ones. Perhaps they'd even started to have feathers then and were able to fly up high enough now and again, over the clouds, I mean to get nice and warm.

That's what evolution is all about. It seems to be an enormous subject. It's not hard to understand how one kind of animal can evolve bigger or smaller to get used to whatever happened to the earth and all the other animals. It's a bit hard though, to understand how a completely new animal suddenly appears.

I saw a giraffe at the zoo last year. It's a very strange animal really and not a bit like anything else I've seen anywhere. I wonder what it was like before it turned into a giraffe.

My grandmother didn't seem to believe in dinosaurs. I showed her some of my pictures. She said, Well if they did exist once, and were so terrible, then God would definitely have destroyed them all, when he was ready to make way for us. That certainly would explain why there aren't any around today, but it doesn't seem a very fair thing to do. Surely they couldn't have all been bad, only the big fierce ones with all those teeth.

I remember asking that Sunday school teacher about dinosaurs and why did God make them, and why were there so many different kinds. Well, she didn't seem to know as much about them as I did. She would only say they were not successful, like we are. I'm not sure about that, and it didn't explain why they were put here in the first place. Anyway, their 140 million years was a lot more than our 3 million, so far. Going by all the news on TV nowadays, I'm not so sure the human race is really so clever and successful and will last for as long as that. If we do then perhaps we'll change into lots of different kinds of human beings, and become all different sizes as well? More than we do now I mean.

Well, perhaps if we don't die out because of global warming or the ozone layer, we'll evolve into something faster and stronger and better too? Human beings today are already a lot more advanced than when they first appeared. I wonder what will come next? I would expect evolution to keep on going. Perhaps some new beings cleverer than we are will appear. I would expect God to want to try something else, and get it more nearly perfect the next time. Then even better the time after that, especially if He wants to keep on improving his own image too.

MINUTES of the second MEETING of the JUNIOR PHILOSOPHICAL SOCIETY on Saturday May 3rd. at 3 pm.

Present: Everyone, same as last time, but Sylvie said I should make a proper list each time.

Minutes of the last Meeting: It seems we should have these read out each time to do things properly. So I did. Then after I did, Joe said he thought we should only have them read out if they're really interesting.

Matters arising: The Golf Club always has this, but Alf said we really don't need it each time. Everybody agreed we could put anything important in at the end if there was anything. After all, we aren't really going to make any decisions about anything. Our meetings are only to discuss interesting subjects. Not at all like that Golf Club.

Subject: EVOLUTION

No, said Alf to Sylvie who asked the first question. This subject is not about how we're all descended from Monkeys. That's what a lot of grown-ups seem to think, but it isn't true.

A long time ago there was one little animal, a mammal, which as we all know means an animal that has its babies born alive and not coming out of an egg that's been laid in a nest and kept warm by sitting on it, like most birds do. Well, it was evolution that turned this little mammal into us, and all the different apes and monkeys. But that doesn't mean we suddenly became human beings. There was what's called our primitive ancestors first. For example there were the Neanderthal Men, called that because I think some of their old skeletons were found in a place called that. They were very hairy and ugly and didn't walk up straight like we do. They probably didn't have to wash so much either.

We're called Homo Sapiens, and that means intelligent humans in the Latin language. But there were lots of different ugly looking ones, who were not so clever, and began more than 40 million years ago at least.

However, a long time before them, in the beginning, after everything hot cooled down enough, life began in the sea with one very simple creature, apparently by accident. It seems that if lightning hits a salty kind of liquid, it makes special chemicals that can turn into something living, called an organism. Some scientists though, think that life may have come here from pieces of a comet, or a meteorite, which landed in the sea. Some fossil looking things have been found in meteorites and it could mean that life came from them and became organisms in the sea.

Sylvie laughed and said some of the older girls at her school had been telling her something interesting about organisms, but it didn't seem to be the same thing. It clearly wasn't, so it certainly isn't going into these minutes anywhere.

Alf continued and said, These organisms only had one cell, like a chicken's egg is today, but they could squash and stretch themselves up and down and along and so move about. Then they changed a little bit and split and became more than one cell joined together and able to do different things. Some of them even started to eat each other, instead of tiny plants like the first ones did so that they could grow. One day, some of them came up on to the land and then kept changing and growing. Then after a long time, some of them became dinosaurs.

Over then next millions of years lots of them got bigger and bigger, and some of them even learned to fly. About then the first little mammals appeared; those warm blood animals that didn't lay eggs like the others. It was a good job they did, so that we could come later on. If not then perhaps we wouldn't have evolved at all! Then one day, or perhaps over a few years, all the dinosaurs disappeared. It was because of some big disaster, like probably an asteroid hitting the earth and making a big cloud that blacked out the sun everywhere and made it very cold. So, all the dinosaurs died out, except for some of the smaller ones and some of those that could fly.

Next, I told the meeting some of what I'd found out before. The smaller ones turned into crocodiles and snakes and lizards. The flying ones finally changed into all the birds that are here today.

Sylvie could hardly believe that a sweet little robin used to be a flying dinosaur. She'd seen pictures of pterodactyl dinosaurs and they were absolutely nothing like a little robin, not even like a vulture!

I said, That kind of flying dinosaur must have died out too, There must have been smaller ones that didn't.

Alf carried on and said, All over the millions of years, before any kind of human beings came, the strongest and fastest creatures always lived the longest. So naturally there were more of them, because they had more time to have more babies. The weaker ones either died out or had to develop to be cleverer and find ways to survive all the terrible dangers that were around in those days. All this development, to be stronger and more able to survive and have more copies of them is what's called The Theory of Evolution. A theory is an idea you're not sure about, until you can prove it. Then it becomes a fact, which I think is what most scientists believe evolution is nowadays. Some religious people still don't believe in Evolution though, even with all the museums you can visit that have the old bones all put together.

Yes, but what makes it all happen, and why do they keep changing, Mike and Joe wanted to know, Sylvie too.

This was something I knew about, so I said, some scientists think it's caused by cosmic rays from space coming in all the time and hitting tiny parts of our body cells, and what's inside them, so that they change a little bit and make things grow differently.

I read about that, Joe said, It's called the DNA. That's what gets changed. It's like all the instructions that tell cells, when they're splitting, what parts of the body to become before we're born. Like a program in a computer. It's how what's in an egg knows whether it should hatch as a chick or a baby crocodile, or whatever.

That's right, I said, Any little change to any part of the DNA code can make the whole organism a little bit different, especially when the next family of baby ones are born. Some of the changes that happen are good and some are not. Organisms that are born with something different and wrong just don't live very long. They die young, or they get eaten up by the stronger ones, and so don't have enough time to have babies. The ones that have changes that are good, and more useful, live longer and have more babies. So, this means there'll be more and more of them as time goes by.

When all this started, after millions of years went by, some of the organisms, and maybe even some of the larger sea creatures that had grown up by then, must have found out that things were getting harder for them in the sea. So they tried moving out on to the land, or perhaps it was because the tide went out and they had to anyway. Some of them grew legs. Those that didn't soon died off, or perhaps they were the ones that went back in the sea again. The ones who did have legs, especially long ones, could run the fastest.

Joe said, They got more food, because they could catch the slower ones easier. But I expect they had to grow some legs before they could go up on to the land?

Not always, argued Sylvie, Snails and snakes don't have legs. Anyway, crabs and lobsters live in the sea and have lots of legs already. They could easily have come up on to the land, any time they wanted.

Or even if they didn't, especially when the sea got rough, said Joe. They'd have got washed up easily.

We all thought about that and then agreed that the sea creatures who already had legs probably were the first to come up on to the land to try it out. But probably not shrimps, if there were any then, because we didn't think they'd be able to stand up properly.

Alf then said, some of them really did go back in again! Some of those who became mammals, the ones whose babies were born alive, like whales and dolphins.

And sea lions and walruses too, said Sylvie, They seem to be half-and-half, living in the sea and on the land.

Mike asked, What about insects then? Did they come out from the sea too? Alf thought they must have done, but he hadn't really found out how insects started, only dinosaurs and mammals, Mike said, Perhaps spiders evolved from crabs, they've got enough legs and things? But what about flies and bees and mosquitoes?

We all thought about that, but nobody had any idea. Then we found we had run out of time. Alf said we should have this subject again another day, it was so big.

I managed to quickly read out the bit in my old notes about giraffes. We decided there were still a lot of things about evolution that we didn't really understand yet. I said I was very interested in giraffes and would try to find out more about how they evolved. For when we did have this subject again.

We all agreed we'd had a very interesting meeting, and were looking forward very much to the next one. It was going to be about aliens and flying saucers! We fixed it to be in three weeks time.

Diary again - Last year, in the summer holidays, I had a terrible toothache and I had to go to the dentist. It started me off thinking about PAIN and why we have it. I looked it up and found out it's meant to protect us from hurting ourselves. Without pain we wouldn't know what's bad for us, until it was too late. I think it is called protection from self-inflicted damage. I'm not sure how that fits in with my toothache. I didn't do anything to make it happen. Not as far as I can remember anyway. Perhaps it evolved to make it easier for us to want to go to the dentist? I bet they didn't have dentists back in the Stone Age times. I wonder if they got toothache in those days? Perhaps it hadn't evolved yet back then? I don't think they had sweets in those days, if that's what caused my toothache. But I don't eat so many really.

Knowing it will hurt quite a bit, certainly stops me from getting a sharp knife and cutting off a piece of my body. Knowing I need the part anyway is just as good as far as I can see. Still, there are always accidents, and perhaps we might not notice we'd done something serious if it didn't hurt at all.

We do seem to be stuck with pain, but I can't help thinking that if we could grow back the parts we damage, that would be a lot more useful. I read that some animals can do it, especially lizards when their tails get pulled off, when something bigger tries to eat them. It's called regeneration, I think, and it seems to me it's a very good idea. Anything you lose by accident, you just grow back again.

It seems an obvious thing really, and my computer thesaurus and spelling checker program is saying that regeneration is the right word. Just think of all the extra bits that we have hanging about, boys anyway. We could easily lose something important in an accident. Knowing it will hurt doesn't seem to stop all the accidents. I really think we should evolve next, able to grow parts back on again. Anyway, perhaps doctors will learn how to do it soon, with genetic engineering.

If we're made in God's image like they say, then He must have fingers and things too, and have to be careful closing doors, like happened to me last week in the bathroom. That really did hurt when I did it, and three of my fingers are still a bit blue. Perhaps there aren't any doors in Heaven. Perhaps they only have them in Hell. I must tell Alf. That could be one of the horrible punishments they have there.

I suppose Heaven must be a place where it's impossible to have any accidents, or pain, or lose things. So they don't need medicine or doctors or any hospitals there. I've never heard anyone say they have cars in Heaven either, so you couldn't get run over. I wonder if they have any animals there? Like pet dogs or cats. There can't be any dangerous animals let loose there anyway, I wonder where they go when they're dead?

I get a pain sometimes when I eat too much. I always enjoy eating a lot at Christmas and at parties, but not always what happens afterwards. I wonder if you can eat too much in Heaven, without getting sick or anything?

I often wonder if God and the angels have all the parts like we have, and eat and drink like we do. You can't tell from any of the pictures or statues in churches. Anyway, Jesus certainly ate things, like we do when we're hungry, and I'm sure he must have got thirsty too. I wanted to ask that Sunday School teacher if they have toilets in Heaven, but I didn't dare to ask her. That seemed to be just the kind of question that would get her all upset again. Anyway I did get her to agree that they must have lots of good things to eat and drink in Heaven. She didn't know about where it was all grown and who cooked everything and where it all went afterwards, or if you had to eat cabbage and sprouts.

MINUTES OF THE EIGHTH MEETING OF THE JUNIOR PHILOSOPHICAL SOCIETY on Saturday November 15th.

Present: Alf Brodie (Chairman)
Alan Charles (Secretary)
Sylvia Richards (Deputy Secretary)
Mike Thomas (Member)
Joseph Bennett (Member)
Fred Clarke (Member)
Joe Bennett (Member)

Minutes of the last meeting: I read them out and everyone was very quiet. We all agreed THE UNIVERSE was a fascinating subject, and must have it again. There were new things being found out about it all the time.

Subject: RELIGION

Alf and I talked a lot about this subject the week before the meeting. I was a bit worried about how Sylvie would feel about it and Joe, our youngest member too. They were both still going to Sunday school.

Alf said he thought it would be very good for them.

I said I thought so too, especially if they learn about what embarrassing questions not to ask the teacher.

I started the meeting saying that, at Sunday school, we were told that if we believed in Jesus we would be saved, but not very much about from what. Except that it was called Eternal Damnation.

Sylvie had to laugh and said, Everyone knows that being saved means you go to Heaven to see God when you die and everything there will be good and wonderful, forever and ever. I think it's best not to know what you'll be saved from, but it must be very bad.

Joe said, It doesn't mean your body actually goes there though does it? It means it's your spirit or your soul, or whatever it's called, that goes. The part of you that knows you're you, and thinks, inside your head. After all, if you got blown up in a war with an atom bomb there wouldn't be anything left of you to be able to go anywhere!

Mike said, But perhaps when you get there, you get a new body so that you can do things again. So that other people there will know it's you, and you'll know it's them. How could anyone know anyone else if you couldn't see them?

I said, If you do get a new body and you died when you were young, I wonder if it goes on growing like before, or if you're very old, it gets young again. I wonder what happens to babies?

We all thought about that.

Then Alf said, If all the babies who die get their bodies back, and carry on growing up, how will their real mothers know them again. Most babies all look the same to me?

Sylvie said, I read that in the old days, mothers had lots more children than today. Lots of them never did live long enough to grow up.

I said, Yes, I read that too. Lots of them had as many as fifteen children. If they were all saved, there must be millions and millions of them in Heaven now. If they didn't carry on growing up, I wonder if they cry a lot, like my little sister does lots of nights? Heaven wouldn't be such a great place to be in if they do, would it? Especially for billions of years.

Fred said, I'm not so sure about what happens after you're dead. If you tread on a beetle it's dead and that's that, but perhaps insects don't think or have anything to carry on afterwards. It must be the same thing if a dog or cat gets run over. Only people are supposed to have an afterlife, and go to Heaven, but only the good ones who have faith.

Mike said, Well if dead people don't go to Heaven then they go to Hell, which is supposed to be a terrible place. There's supposed to be another place too which is about half way! But what about all the people in the world who've never even heard of Jesus? Like those who lived before Him, and those who have lived since then in far away countries where they have different religions, anyway? How could they ever become saved? There must be billions of them, and what about all the Stone Age people, and the ones before them?

We all thought about that.

I heard an important priest on the radio once, I said. He was asked exactly that question and said, Yes, people will be saved if they were good in their life. It's only if you know about Jesus and God and don't believe that makes you not saved.

That doesn't seem right, Mike said, because it sounds like it's safer to be good and not to know anything about him.

Alf said, It means the missionaries or teachers, who go there, must be ones who will do a really good job in other countries where they have different religions. If not, then the people there won't change and then they won't be saved. That doesn't really sound very fair to me.

Everything that's important to learn always depends on how good the teachers are, I said, But I don't think ours explain these kind of things to us very well, do they? The Bible doesn't say anything like enough about all the scientific things we like to talk about at our meetings. There's absolutely nothing in it about dinosaurs either!

Sylvie said, How could it? The people who wrote it all down didn't know about science in those days. They could only explain things by what they knew about the world they lived in, as it was then.

Yes, I said, and their part of the world was very small then with not many people about to discuss things. It took them days to get to anywhere else. If you look at a map of Israel you can see how small it is. They couldn't know how big the world really is.

Alf said, But today we know how small it really is. A tiny planet going round a small sun in just one galaxy, and there's billions of those. Like Fred said last time, how could it really have all been created just for us? Anyway, how could anything written down in those days, about creation or evolution, seem right to us today, when they thought their world was the center of everything, and it was all made just for them.

Do you think it was the same with all the different religions in the world, asked Mike. I mean the ones that started a long time ago. Not the new ones they keep thinking up and then want to kill themselves, like we hear about on the news sometimes.

I said, I think all the other main religions in the world are at least two thousand years old now. So I suppose the people who started them didn't know very much about science either. How could they?

Alf said, What I don't understand is why everyone religious is sure they have the only true meaning and understanding of everything.

And they still fight and kill anyone who doesn't agree with them, I said. They can't all be right, can they? So why can't they stop and think about things like we try to do.

Mike said, Perhaps one day they will, when the aliens come.

Alf said, It's all down to where you were born. Children grow up to have the same religion as their parents, just like we said about politics last time. You grow up with the family religion, just like your parents did.

I think we should be taught about all the different religions equally, said Mike. Then we could decide which one was the best when we were properly grown up. But there are so many. I wonder which one would really turn out to be the best?

It's possible perhaps none of them would, I said, and Fred said he agreed with me.

Sylvie said, How can you say that? You have to believe in something. Everybody must. It's not natural to believe in nothing.

Joe said he agreed with her.

I said, I didn't say you had to believe in nothing. There're plenty of other things to believe in. Nothing to do with miracles or magic or anything like that. Why can't you just believe in what can be proved to be true? You can keep your mind open for anything new or old to be proved true as new facts are found out. I think that's what's called being an agnostic is about.

That's right, said Alf, They keep on finding out new things in science and then have to change some of the ideas they had before. So that kind of believing has to keep changing all the time. If you're not sure about things then that is called being an agnostic. If you believe in nothing at all, then that's what being an atheist is about. Like the communists in Russia used to be.

Fred said, It seems to me that if you stick to one of the religious kind of religions then it shouldn't change. Everything about it comes from what's written in the special book for that religion, made a long time ago.

I said, So there can't be anything really new about it, left to be found out, not like science. But some people do think about it and sometimes in history they didn't, or even today they don't agree with the way it's being done. Then they start a new version of the religion they started with. Yet it's still the same book they all read before and got their ideas from.

We all decided it was very hard to be really sure about some of the things we're told about, to do with religion. Even Sylvie, and we all agreed we didn't expect to get much help about it from any grown-ups. It was all back to having faith again, and believing in what grown-ups say we should believe in, if we wanted to be saved.

Alf said, I think it's all about human behavior too. It makes a lot of sense to always be good to other people, and never hurt them, so that they're always good to you back.

I said, From everything I've heard and read about, most of the different religions believe that. They say you should love your neighbors, and forgive them for whatever they do to you, no matter how bad it is.

Yes, but perhaps it means only to other people with the same religion as you, Mike said.

Joe suddenly wanted to know what we all thought God looked like. He'd seen different pictures in a book his granny gave him one Christmas. . Some showed Him like a big white light, and another like a bush or a tree on fire. Others showed Him looking like a kind old man.

Mike said, If we were made in His image, then surely He must look like us.

Alf and I had thought about this a lot before the meeting, and I had written out some Notes about what we had decided. I started to read them out but Sylvie stopped me and said it was too late for all that as she and Joe had to be home earlier today. So that ended the meeting.

Alf said I should put the notes I didn't finish reading out into our records, even if we didn't give them to any of the others. So here they are ... the writing looks different because I brought it in from a different place in my computer.

What does God look like?

1. *He must have just lived in Heaven, or somewhere else, before He created the universe. So perhaps it's how things are there that would have made Him like He looks. Even if He created Heaven too, He must have been somewhere else before that!*

2. *He must be able to travel a lot faster than light to keep in touch with everything going on just in our galaxy, even faster to get around all the others billions in the universe. That might mean He needs to be a special shape, as well as to have the enormous power you'd need to be able to get around instantly. But He must also have ways to stop time from slowing down and not get infinitely big, which are things that Einstein said must happen when you get to the speed of light.*

3. *With no planets to move about on and so no light or any air to breathe, before he created everything, He wouldn't really need to have eyes and ears, arms and legs like ours. Unless Heaven is on some planet, with air and a sun, in another dimension or something.*

4. *To be able to hear our prayers though, however many millions of light years away He happens to be at the time, must need some kind of instant telepathy. We know there can't be any sounds in space.*

5. *Perhaps He changed, or even created himself, to look like the human beings he wanted to create when He was ready.*

   The latest information we've found is that the universe is about 14 billion years old, and we've only been around in it for about 4 million years. The dinosaurs were around for at least 35 times that! Thinking about all the news on TV it's hard to believe that human beings will last that long anyway.

Alf said his big brother thinks it's more likely that God was invented in man's image! By some clever person, thousands of years ago, who wanted to control people and have a good life as a priest or something. We must see what the others think about that idea at our next meeting.

Well, we didn't, so it was Any Other Business instead:

We agreed not to tell our parents about what we talk about at our meetings so we don't get them embarrassed or anything. We believe they think we just play games on my computer. We decided we would talk about time travel next time.

Yes, I nearly forgot to put in that Fred brought me some blank cassettes for my tape recorder which I use it to record our meetings. Listening to them later makes it easy to see what to put into these minutes. We all agreed I must never forget to erase them afterwards.

More thoughts from my diary - I read that everything there is, always stays on our planet because it's so big. Like water for example. The sun warms it, and evaporates it, and it goes up and forms clouds. Then the clouds rain and it comes down again. All the water on the planet just keeps going up, and sideways if it's windy, and then down again. All the time, wherever, none of it is ever lost. Only the very light gases which don't weigh as much as air, like hydrogen, get lost out into space. Everything else always stays behind, because of gravity. So everything all the people in olden days drank must still be going around today.

I suddenly realized we must still be drinking some of it. So somewhere, all the drops of water and wine that Jesus, and all the people then, drank must still be going around too. Inside people then out again, and up into clouds and then down again. Over and over again. It all must be everywhere by now, but very diluted. That's no different to what they have to do in a space station. The water they take up has to be recycled. So our planet is like space station, but a lot bigger, and with lots and lots more people.

That's very interesting, but it is not very easy to talk about things like diluted old water, going round and round... to grown-ups.

My parents don't seem to know much about space. All the really interesting things in life seem to me to be like that. I told Alf Brodie what I'd realized and he laughed. Now we know why it's called Holy Water, he said. He told me he saw the vicar get some out of an ordinary tap, to fill the font before that last twins Christening service we had to sing at. Alf said, He only seemed to say some special words to himself when some of it went all over one of his shoes.

I've been reading a lot more books and programs about astronomy lately. They say there are more than a hundred billion suns in our galaxy. That's a really enormous number. We can't be the only ones with a planet you can live on. What's more, there are billions and billions of other galaxies! It's hard to really appreciate how big it all must be. There must be an awful lot of planets, probably with life on them, for God to look after.

MINUTES OF THE THIRD MEETING OF THE JUNIOR PHILOSOPHICAL SOCIETY on Saturday May 24th., supposed to be starting at 3 pm, but it was more like 3.30.

Present: Alf (Chairman), Alan (Secretary), Sylvie (Assistant Secretary), Mike and Joe (Members), Fred (New Member)

Alf started us off this time by introducing our new member Fred Clarke who is eleven and a science-fiction fan. He heard about our Club and wanted to join. He's not sure if he can always come though because he lives alone with his mother and has to help with things in the house some weekends.

Next, I read out the minutes of the last meeting. Everybody agreed with them, so then we started on this new subject.

Subject: ALIENS AND UFOs

What a super subject we all agreed, in the end anyway, especially Mike who wanted it recorded as his choice, and even Sylvie who said she really would have preferred The Future next, especially Global Warming. After only a little argument, we got started, with Joe wanting to know if aliens are here already, and if not then when are they coming? He was really looking forward to seeing some.

Mike said he'd seen quite a lot of people who could be aliens. Even more last week, since he knew this was going to be the subject today.

Sylvie laughed and said perhaps one of her teachers at school could be an alien. He didn't wear normal untidy clothes like the other teachers and he had a very funny voice. He always wore a tie and a brown jacket and dark green trousers, every day all through the year.

We all agreed this was certainly strange, even if she was not being serious..

Alf said Sylvie should tell us at each meeting if she noticed anything else unusual about him.

Joe suggested perhaps his clothes were all part of him, especially if he was a shape-shifter alien, like we see on TV sometimes.
Joining in, I said, But if he was then surely he could change his colours any time he wanted?

Joe said, But perhaps he was only programmed back on his own planet, before he came to us, just to have one selection of clothes?

That was enough of that! We talked about what real aliens might really look like. Sylvie thought a lot of the ones on TV were really silly. They all had horrible spotty faces and terrible hairstyles. You could see they were just human beings dressed up to look like aliens and monsters.

I said, I'd read that it was not likely that real aliens would look anything like us. Evolution was all by chance and about opportunities for what happened by luck, to change and then survive better and for longer and then have more babies.

Say that again said Alf, so I did.

Anyway, I said, Even if life evolved on another planet somewhere exactly the same as ours, it didn't mean that the intelligent life on it would have to look like us. The way it developed would be just only by chance, like I said before.

Fred said, Perhaps in another few million years, if there is any intelligent life left on this planet, it won't be very much like us either.

Joe said, Perhaps all the ants will take over from us, if we die out for any reason, after they've got a lot bigger. They'd have to get bigger to have big enough brains to be really intelligent. Insects could take over next. Some of them are clever already aren't they?

No, that's not likely, said Fred, As you get bigger your weight goes up faster. That's easy to prove in mathematics. A very big ant couldn't have strong enough legs to walk about. But they could grow bigger brains I suppose.

How about spiders asked Joe, they can be a lot bigger than the ones we get at home ... and with thick hairy legs too. I think he said that to scare Sylvie, who hates spiders. It did too.

I said, I thought machines and computers would be more likely to take over. They could live on and on and mend each other and get really intelligent. I was sure, seeing how far away all the stars are, and the years and years it would take to get to here, the only way aliens could visit us is if they were machines.

How do we know for how long aliens can live, asked Joe? If they're cleverer than we are then perhaps they've found ways to live a long time. Anyway, it also depends on how fast their spaceships can go. Perhaps faster than the speed of light, in hyperspace.

I said, Yes, but if that's not possible, like some scientists think, then they'd have to live a very long time even to come to us from the nearest star, never mind the other side of just our galaxy. I've read stories where spaceships were so big people lived all their lives on them.

Teaching their children how to run the spaceship, then their children teaching their children, and so on. They'd be traveling all the time until they found a nice planet to live on. It's hard to believe, but that's the only way they could do it, I said, With all the space they would have to travel through to come such a long way. I know they do it in stories and films and TV, but going faster than light in hyperspace, or anything like that, might never be possible, according to lots of scientists, especially Einstein.

Fred said, Lots of stars though are nearer than that to us. I read scientists have already found what looks like planets going round some of them. At about half the speed of light I think it wouldn't take more than 10 years for aliens to get from some of the nearer ones to us.

Sylvie wanted to know why they'd want to come and visit us anyway.

Joe said, Perhaps because our TV after nine o'clock is better than theirs. If they were not more than ten light years away, they would have already been watching our TV by now.

I said, Yes but it would be ten years old programs! Television and radio all travel as fast as light. Anyway, perhaps their own planet was in danger and they wanted somewhere else to live. They'd come with their own plants and animals and everything they'd need for the journey and for when they finally arrive and set up their new homes.

Alf said he read a book once where someone thought that was how we came here. The spaceship crashed, perhaps in the sea near some land, but just enough people and some animals escaped to start the human race. The idea was that we are aliens really, but don't remember that or how we came here in the first place. When we got going, being cleverer, we killed off all the Stone Age people and soon took over. Perhaps we didn't have any primitive ancestors here after all? We had them somewhere else!

Sylvie said she didn't believe that. Aliens have never been here yet, but perhaps they will one day.

I said, No, I'm not sure. Perhaps they never will. Perhaps aliens are something like us and get ill and have pollution and global warming and bad things like that. So that they die out or kill each other before they get really started on space travel to other stars and galaxies.

Fred said, How about if they didn't have those problems, but their star was going to explode or something? That could happen, then they would want to build spaceships to rescue everyone.

I said, Perhaps we'll have to do that one day? I read that a giant asteroid or comet could hit us and make life on this planet impossible for us, like they say it happened to the dinosaurs. I read one is going to come very close in the year 2028!

Mike wanted to know how many people could you get in a spaceship. Everybody in the world certainly couldn't go.

I tried working it out on my computer. I said, if it was a really big one, about a mile long, you could easily make it like a city with about 100,000 people in it. So you'd need 10 giant spaceships for every million people.

Mike said, How many people in the world would really want to go?

Alf said, All of them, if they knew it was going to happen, except perhaps a lot of the really old people. The ones you often hear about who never want to leave home even if they know there's going to be a flood or something.

I said, There's about 60 million people here in England and Scotland and Wales, so we'd need 600 giant spaceships just to take all those!

Alf said, I think that there are about five thousand million people in the world now, so that makes fifty thousand spaceships altogether.

We all thought about that.

Joe said, It's impossible, there wouldn't be enough time to build that many, especially if it was a big asteroid that was coming.

I agreed and said, I read it took 3 years just to get the first Concorde ready for supersonic testing, and that was made on the ground. Giant spaceships can only be built in space or perhaps on the moon where they wouldn't weigh so much.

It would be impossible to save everybody, Alf said. Perhaps there would only be time to build one big one. Think how many shuttles would be needed to put all the parts up into space just for one.

People would have to be selected to go. Sylvie said, Like the Prime Minister and the Royal Family, and some scientists to make it all work.

Joe said, The spaceship designer would have to go too. He'd be the best one to know how to work everything. I think I'd like to design spaceships when I grow up.

Mike said, I bet all the politicians in the government would be the ones to go too. All those people with all their families would soon fill it up. I think I'll be a Cabinet Minister when I grow up, then I would be sure to go too.

Let's get back to Aliens and talk about UFOs now, Alf said. Lots of people say they've seen them, and a lot say they've been inside them. They were kidnapped and taken inside a flying saucer to have all kinds of medical operations done on them.

What kind of operations, asked Sylvie, very quietly.

Alf said, Some people said they were put on to a table and then opened up so the aliens could see what human beings are like inside. They must have been closed up again though I suppose, to be able to come back and talk about it.

Sylvie didn't want to know any more about that. But Joe said, I bet it's like we'd want to do to any aliens we kidnapped if they came here, or when we went to them one day.

Mike said, Do you think aliens have different religions just like human beings do?

Fred said, I expect they do, and if they do visit us perhaps they'll try to make us change to their religion.

Joe said, Perhaps they'll kill us if we don't want to change. Anyway, perhaps they'll want to make us into slaves, or even want to eat us if we don't taste too bad for them, after we're cooked.

Mike said, If they do then we will have to become freedom fighters.

We'll all have to be terrorists against the aliens, Joe agreed.

Everybody cheered, except Sylvie.

I said, I still think machines are more likely to be what will visit us. I read a story once about a big alien spaceship coming here. It turned out to be an intelligent machine. The whole thing, all of it, and made millions of years before it came to our solar system. In the story, it decided we were not clever enough to be interesting to it, so it just carried on to look somewhere else. We couldn't do anything about it, because it was too enormous and we didn't have any ideas how to stop it. Our astronauts had to get off it again before it went, except for one who got killed in an accident on it.

Fred said, Perhaps one like that will visit us one day. I wonder if we'll be able to communicate with it, if it does. I wonder what it would tell us about itself and where it came from. Think what we could learn from it, if it let us,

Joe said, If it doesn't want to destroy us first, I expect we could learn to talk to it. Our biggest computers should be able to talk to it by then. They' re getting faster and cleverer every day now.

We all thought about that. Then Joe said he was afraid our computers and robots might start working with any alien machines that did visit us. Perhaps they would help them take over our planet.

We all thought about that too. Then Fred said, We'll have to put a computer virus in our systems, which only switches on if they do try that.

Alf said, As long as they're not clever enough to disable it first. Anyway, time's up now. We'll discuss what might happen in the future when we have that subject another time. I think Alan should be the one to introduce it.

Yes please, I said. I've already started getting some notes done about what might happen in the future. It's a very important subject, especially for us when we're grown up.

There wasn't any other business again, I forgot to put that in last time!

Back to my diary now ... all the astronomy books I've read say all the suns and galaxies are all moving away from each other, faster and faster. That means it must take longer each time if you want to get from one of them to another and back again. I'm sure I'd get fed up with that if I had to do it.

Then there's that big problem to do with the speed of light. Einstein found out that nothing we know can go faster than that, it seems. So unless God can, or somehow knows how to be in lots of different places at the same time, He doesn't stand a chance of looking after everything all the time. Traveling at the speed of light sounds very fast, but it isn't anything like fast enough..!

It would take millions and millions of years for God just to cross over our galaxy. Think how long it must take to get to any of the others and then go across them too!

He must want to know what's going on in any of them. After all, if He created them, then he must want to worry about them too. Yet That Sunday School teacher said He's always with us and hears us, and knows everything we think and say and do. That must mean everybody, all at the same time, and every planet in every galaxy in the universe. The trouble is, even if thoughts travel as fast as light, then he'd only hear what was being said millions of years ago, if he was in another galaxy at the time.

It seems to me that He must have made the universe in a very complicated way to be able to do that. Perhaps it's all to do with traveling into the fourth dimension, or what's called hyper-space in lots of science-fiction stories? Well, all the different kinds of Enterprise star-ships on TV certainly go faster than light when they want to do it. Occasionally they go backwards and forwards in time too, so maybe that's the answer. If God can travel through time, then he can always get to see anybody at any time eventually. But the traveling bit must be very boring with all those enormous distances to cover. Perhaps he's really only interested in us, or the latest things he's doing. Perhaps it's his hobby to experiment with all kinds of life. From what we're taught about in History and all we see on the TV News, I think perhaps human beings could be an experiment that's going wrong a lot of the time.

MINUTES OF THE SEVENTH MEETING OF THE JUNIOR PHILOSOPHICAL SOCIETY on Saturday 18th. October.

Present: Alf Brodie (Chairman)
Alan Charles (Secretary)
Sylvia Richards (Deputy Sec.)
Mike Thomas (Member)
Joseph Bennett (Member)
Fred Clarke (Member)

Minutes of the last Meeting: Sylvie said, Let's take them as read! She said this was what you always had to say when nobody was interested to hear them.

Subject: THE UNIVERSE AND CREATION

Alf started us off. He said this is a very big subject, which will need at least two meetings. Alan is going to introduce it.

I said, It is a very, very big subject. All the stars you can see in the sky without a telescope are part of our own galaxy. But that's not anything like all of them. On a very dark and clear night you can just see what's called the Milky Way, going right across the sky. That's the light from all across one part of our galaxy, looking in to the middle of it. Just one arm of it, like you see on a Catherine wheel on firework night. It's really billions of stars so far away that they just look like a glow in the sky and not little dots of light at all. Yet lots of them are bigger than our sun, and lots of them are doubles. Two stars turning round each other.

Now with all the big new telescopes, and especially the one in space, scientists can see millions and millions of other galaxies, everywhere they look. Some are like ours but lots of them are bigger or smaller, or like a ball of stars and all kinds of shapes. They keep on finding new things when they look in different places. The problem is the more powerful a telescope is, the more it can see in just a tiny part of the sky. So it takes ages and ages to see all the tiny parts of the sky, one at a time. Everywhere they look they see more galaxies. I think the latest number is now more than 200 billion.

What's important about them is that they are all moving away from each other. If you put their positions and speeds into a computer then run it backwards, it turns out that they must have all been in the same place before they started moving away from each other. So it seems it was an enormous explosion that started everything off, called the Big Bang.

Mike said, That must have been the biggest bang there ever was. It certainly must have been enormous, but it's hard to believe that everything was all in one spot. How could it have been? It must have been a very big spot. And what made it all explode anyway?

Alf said, It might have happened before. It could be what made everything explode, because gravity pulled it all back together again from an explosion that happened before that. I read that some scientists think it goes on forever and ever and always did, and always will, without any beginning. Exploding, when everything comes back together again, then slowing down because of gravity until everything stops, and then coming back together again. Then exploding again and all happening again. Over and over again, always the same thing.

That's seems an impossible idea to me, said Sylvie. If everything was always there then God didn't have to create it. How could it have always been there? There must have been a first Big Bang in the beginning.

Joe said, Yes, and we all know the Bible says God made it all happen in six days and then had a rest, to make up the first week. But he must have always been there before that?

Fred said, But there's nothing in the Bible about what it was all like before God created it, or how long it was before he did decide to create it. Is there?

I said, I didn't think there was, and seven days couldn't mean anything real when there was nothing there. It needed our planet going round and round to give the days and how long they were. You can't have days without a planet first, going round a sun. Anyway, the latest story in science is that our Sun and planets are about 5 billion years old, but the Big Bang was about 14 billion years ago. A billion is a thousand of millions, and that's an awful lot.

We all agreed that it was an enormous number because a million is a thousand of thousands, and that's a big enough number just for a start.

I told them about the 47 super-years way of looking at everything, and how the Bible story of Creation was really all people in those days could understand.

Alf said, They even thought the world was flat and you'd fall off the edge if you went far enough out to sea.

Mike said, How could they think anything else, without telescopes and satellites and space travel, and all the scientists we have today to find out all these things. They didn't have any scientific instruments.

I don't see how anyone who lived near the sea could think the world was flat, Fred said. If you stand on the beach and look across to an island, you can't see its beach or anything low down on it, because it's under the curve of the earth. I've seen the same thing when a boat goes away from the harbor. When you're standing on the sea wall you can see it slowly getting lower and lower down until just before it disappears, you can only see the masts. It's just the same wherever you are, and whatever way you look, so the earth must be a big ball.

Well perhaps in those days nobody important noticed, I said. Anyway, the really important thing is the time it takes for the light from a star to get here to us, so that we see it. For lots of them it's taken millions and millions and millions of years.

Alf said, So we are really seeing them just as they were when the light started off from them. That means they could look quite different now if we could be there with them. They could even be in a different place from how they look now.

Say that again, we all said. So he did.

Mike said, Perhaps the ones farthest away have already slowed down. Perhaps they're already on the way back again for the next Big Bang.

We all went very quiet thinking about this.

Then Sylvie said, wouldn't we see them coming back too? As they got nearer to us, the light wouldn't have so far to go.

Joe said, perhaps two stars we see sometimes are really the same one. One going away and the other one the same one coming back again.

Mike said, I don't think so, everything I've read says all the ones we can see are all moving away from us, faster and faster. Anyway, I don't think we have to worry about the next Big Bang, it couldn't happen again for millions and millions more years. Could it?

I said, Don't worry, there's much more chance of a comet or asteroid hitting us before that, and destroying everything. Like happened to all those dinosaurs.

Sylvie said, Oh great, I do feel better now, knowing that. I don't want to hear about any more terrible things that might happen to us.

I said, Let's talk more about the speed of light. Einstein said you can't ever go faster than that, how ever big you make your rocket engine or whatever you use. You can use as much power as you want, but you can only get closer to it. Another problem is you also get bigger, because all the extra energy you use does that to you instead of making you go faster. Time slows down too, so everything takes longer.

Sylvie said, That sounds very strange, and hard to believe. What about God then? If the universe is so big, he must be able to travel fast enough to go to any part of it to see what's happening. Are you saying His speed makes him big too?

We all thought about that, and I remembered some of my old diary notes.

Then I said, Perhaps that's why he doesn't often answer all the people who pray on a Sunday. Or those who are in danger from an earthquake. How could he hear everything if he's busy in some other galaxy. How fast can prayers go, so he hears them?

Alf said, But I remember our Sunday school teacher saying He's everywhere and hears and knows all we say and do. So, He must be bigger than the universe, to be everywhere. But he'd have to be here in the atmosphere to hear prayers, because sounds don't travel in space. It's a vacuum, everyone know that. Anyway, it's hard enough to hear my mum calling me for dinner through our new double-glazing.

Sylvie said, I think He does it with telepathy then, because people often don't pray out loud. Perhaps thoughts can go faster than light?

We all thought about that.

Then Joe said, Well ours didn't that time we tried it, remember?

I said, It seems to me that the universe is so enormous, it's impossible to be in every part of it at the same time. So it's one of those Faith things again. It doesn't seem possible, but we have to believe it must be, if we want to be religious. Anyway, if God can go faster than light, then perhaps one day we'll find out how to do it too.

Joe said, And if one day we find out how to do it, then we'll know He already did.

I said, Let's get back to how big the universe is. I don't think ordinary grown-ups really understand how big it all is, and it's hard enough for us. I was reading before this meeting that just our galaxy is over one hundred thousand light years across. That means it would take 100,000 years for light to go right across it. That means those stars in it that are farthest away are right now are in a different place to how they look, and the ones nearest are also in a different place now, but not so different as the ones that are furthest away.

Yes, Okay, I said, I'll say that again, and I did. Then once more slowly for Joe. I drew a little drawing to explain it better.

Mike said, That seems to me to mean that we can't see exactly how a galaxy that's not flat on to us really looks. Our sun is where it is to us alright, but every star we look at that's farther and farther away is more and more not where it really is now.

Joe said, This is getting too hard for me to think about. All I know is that it's all so big and enormous, with all the millions and millions and millions of other galaxies.

Fred said, Yes, and we can't be very important on this little planet, can we? How could it have all been created just for us? How could that be true? I don't think God could have pressed the Big Bang button just for us to come along millions and millions of years later after everything else.

I said, That's how I think about it too. How could it all be for us? Even if we last the next million years exploring it, even going faster than light, we'll never be able to see very much of it at all. Human beings just don't live long enough.

Sylvie was very quiet, just thinking. Joe was too.

Alf said, How about if it was really made for some aliens somewhere else who do live a very long time then?

Fred said, Perhaps they even made it for themselves. You never know, maybe some kinds of life can do anything. One thing I'd like to know is, what actually is life? If you tread on an ant … it's dead. Just before that, it wasn't. What is it that's gone? Something like electricity?

Nobody had any idea about that.

Fred said, Anything moving, that's not machinery, is usually alive. Anything dead definitely isn't. But alive things don't always move do they? What about plants? And seeds too. I read they can last for thousands of years and then still grow if they are planted and watered properly. They always seem to look dead, but they're not.

Sylvie said, My dad and I planted lots of grass seeds on our lawn, but only a few of them came up. The rest must have died or have been dead when he bought them. I saw them before we planted them and they all looked the same to me.

Joe said, And what about an egg. It certainly isn't moving when a chicken lays it … but a little chick grows inside it, and that definitely is alive. What is it that gets added to make it alive … and when does it happen?

We all thought about that.

Then Alf ended by saying that, Clearly life must be some kind of force that switches on to start things off and then switches off to stop them when they die.

Any other business: We had some time left this week, so I looked up the speed of light again. It's about 186,000 miles in one second. That's unbelievable fast! Space Rockets haven't gone much faster than 7 miles a second yet. Fred said, How could you make sure you wouldn't hit anything in the way, traveling that fast, if you could go that fast, or even near to it?

We all agreed and found out too that Radar can't go any quicker than light, so how could you ever see, or even be able to tell, what was in the way of where you were going. It sounded very dangerous. We decided you'd have to have some very good maps of space, especially as everything keeps moving to different places all the time.

I can't see how you could ever have enough time to make any maps, Joe said. It would be safer to go slower, but then you wouldn't see very much.

We all agreed this had been a very interesting meeting. The universe was much bigger than we had realized before. We thought too that it was much more enormous than most grown-ups ever realized. We even decided it was most probably a lot bigger than we, or anyone, could ever imagine it was, especially all the grown-ups we knew.

Diary again ... That brings me back to that idea about us not being made perfect. I often remember my Dad said to my Mum once that if she expected him to be perfect, she might not like it in the end. He said if he grew to be perfect, then she probably wouldn't be good enough for him! That did it! She wouldn't talk to him for nearly 3 days after that. I had to pass them their messages to each other, even though I was sure they could hear each other telling me to do it.

Sometimes grown-ups seem to behave like some children I know, but who are quite a lot younger than I am!

The vicar in our church seems to be sure that he can pass messages to God. Sometimes after he's asked specially for something, he seems to stop and listen for the answer. I asked him once if God always hears and always does answer our prayers. He said yes, of course, but sometimes God's answer is No. That does seem only fair really, if we want it to be nice day just for some outing like a picnic. If it's been dry for weeks all the farmers need it to rain. Food for the Nation must be more important, so the answer has to be No to our picnic. We should only plan to have picnics when we hear farmers have started to pray for the rain to stop.

I heard my dad say his boss at work thinks he's God. Well, some of the time anyway, I think he means. It must be very nice to be a God like that, and be paid the most money. Especially if everyone must be grateful to you when the answer is Yes, but have to be understanding, when the answer is No,

I remember reading about an earthquake they had in Japan, back in the year 1923 I think it was. About 130,000 people got killed, all at the same time. That's really a terrible lot of people. They couldn't have all been bad, just like I thought about the dinosaurs when they all went. I suppose the ones that didn't get killed were very thankful. I expect they thanked God for protecting them.

The ones who did get killed, all 130,000 of them, must have found it very hard to understand why the answer to their prayers was, Sorry Not Today. Not that they could hear the answer. Anyway, I don't think Japanese people have the same God to listen that we do over here, in Europe and America. It seems we often get earthquakes in Europe too. I read there was one not so long ago where 30,000 people all got killed. I know it was wrong to think it, but I couldn't help wondering how much praying they were all doing when that happened. I expect they were a bit fed up when they got to Heaven, or wherever. I wonder when the next big one will come and where it will be, and how many will be killed?

MINUTES OF THE NINTH MEETING OF THE JUNIOR PHILOSPHICAL SOCIETY on Saturday January 17th.

Present: Alf Brodie (Chairman)
Alan Charles (Secretary)
Sylvia Richards (Deputy Secretary)
Mike Thomas (Member)
Joseph Bennett (Member)
Fred Clarke (Member)

Minutes of the last Meeting: Before the meeting, Sylvie and Joe had decided they didn't want me to read them out, but they didn't want to say why. After a little while we agreed it would leave more time for today's subject, so I didn't.

Subject: TIME TRAVEL

Mike started us off this time and said, This is a subject I really can't believe in. I mean going back in time anyway.

Fred agreed, If it could be done, we would have seen people doing it by now. They'd be like tourists coming back to our time to see us and how everything was.

It depends, Alf said. Perhaps they do come back, but only to watch important events. There are never any important events in our town, so why would we ever see them?

Mike said, There would be something about it in the newspapers and on TV if they did come. But not if the government made it into a secret like some people say they do about UFOs and aliens coming here already, like we discussed last time.

I said, I don't see how time travel could ever be possible. Suppose we had a bottle of Cola on that table there and left it for a few hours before we drank it all up. Then we got into a time machine and went back to five minutes before we drank it. It would all be there again, so we could drink it all up again. Then if we went back further, another five minutes more, it would still be there again, so we could drink it up again.

You could keep on doing it right back to when it was first put on the table, Sylvie said. Even thousands of times if you left it long enough in the first place. That's just silly!

What makes it really impossible, I said, Is that if you came forward in time again from the beginning, you'd see yourself drinking it over and over again.

Alf said, How about going back to a horse race meeting, knowing who'd won. You could bet money over and over again and always win.

Fred said, That's a good way to spot time travelers. Watch out for the very rich people, the ones who always win, and that'll be them!

Going back to that Cola, said Joe, if you didn't drink it you could take it and put it in the time machine. Then each time you went back further you could fill up the time machine with full bottles. You could start a drinks shop!

I said, I've got another idea. You could keep going back into a big shop with the same pocket money and buy lots of things with it again and again.

Fred suddenly laughed and said, You could even keep getting on to the end of a queue where everyone in front was you. All with the same money!

Sylvie laughed too and said, And you could all even give your pocket money to the first you in the front of the queue, to buy something really expensive!

After she had to say that again, Alf said, How about building up a very big savings bank account by keep going back to the Post Office with the same birthday money? It would be easy to become a millionaire and then go back to pay for the time machine in the first place!

Fred said, Great and what about all the times you came back to the same time. How many of you would keep getting out of the same machine?

After that we all agreed the idea of Time Travel going back was really silly.

Then, Mike said, How about if you were not really there? Perhaps you can go back in time if you have to become invisible first, or be like a ghost.

Fred said, I think it could only work if you can't change anything that's already happened. It mustn't be possible to go back and have an accident.

Joe said, I'd like my dad to go back to last Saturday with the numbers that won the Lottery. But just think what could happen if you went back and met your mum and dad before they had you?

Alf said, It might put them off having you, then what would happen?

Mike said, Well, if Joe suddenly disappears, it means he'll grow up to be a mad scientist and build a time machine and go back to see his mum and dad. Maybe one of them would have heart failure at seeing him?

Look, I said, I think he's beginning to go already!

We had some fun with Joe then, pretending he'd suddenly disappeared.

After Joe had stopped being worried, Fred said, If you went back in time to another dimension, perhaps you could just look in to our world and see what happened, but not be able to do anything about it. Perhaps you would be invisible to everybody if you could do that.

Joe wanted to know what other dimensions really were? Nobody seemed to really know so finally Fred said he'd try to find out a bit more about them ready for another meeting.

Then Sylvie said, I think we were right when we said Time Travel to the past was just not possible. But what about going to the future? That couldn't upset anything, could it?

Alf said, That's more likely possible, as long as you don't come back, because that would be time travel to the past again. Perhaps if you could be put to sleep and frozen solid, then one day in the future you could be defrosted to wake up again. Deep frozen things don't seem to grow older if they stay cold enough and solid.

Sylvie wasn't so sure about that. She said, So why do they have sell-by dates on frozen things then, if they would keep for years and years?

Joe said, My mum says it's so they can change the prices. But perhaps if you did manage to freeze a human being properly you would need a defrost-by-date?

I said, I read it's not possible yet because our body cells break up if we deep freeze them. The water inside them gets bigger when it freezes and breaks the thin skin around the cells. I read it works better if you can freeze things very fast and very, very cold. You can't freeze a human being very fast though because you can't get the cold to be all the way through at the same time. Even if you could almost do it, then it would still be the cells in the middle that would get broken up. The trouble is, human beings are made of 70% water. You really need to take that out first, or some of it anyway. Like they do with freeze-dried peas. They keep for ages and you can put the water back anytime.

It's like the pipes in our roof, Mike said, If they freeze up in a cold winter, they really get broken when it freezes. It's only when they get defrosted again that the ice inside them turns to water and comes out all over the ceiling. Then some grown-ups say the pipes have just burst, which isn't right.

Joe said, I don't want to go into the future then. I wouldn't want to be frozen and then to have all my 70 per cent water come out all over the floor, when I'm defrosted. I don't fancy being freeze-dried either!

Alf said, It might be good for you Joe.

We all laughed, except Joe, because he is a bit tubby.

I said, There's another way to go into the future. Einstein found it out from his Theory of Relativity. If you go very fast, nearly up to the speed of light, time slows down, but only for you. Then when you come back again, you find that everybody you left behind will have got a lot older than you, depending on how long you were away traveling that fast.

Sylvie had heard this before, but still couldn't believe it. She said, You mean, if your big brother went off in a fast rocket for long enough, he'd come back younger than you?

Yes, I said. It's not just a theory, it's been proved. Some scientists tried it with a special clock in a rocket going round the earth in orbit. They kept a second one, exactly the same on the ground and started them going together. Then they checked them both each time the rocket went around and around. The one in orbit definitely went slower.

Sylvie wanted to know how they could be sure both the clocks were exactly the same?

I said they were atomic clocks, so they always must be the same, whatever.

Mike said, I'd want to check everything by getting the one in orbit back on the ground, then putting the other one in the rocket, to go into orbit and see if they both ended up the same. And what about how long it takes for the time signal in the rocket to be sent back down to the ground again?

That started a noisy argument, especially when Alf said, The one in orbit before, would be going normal again on the ground. They'd have to set the time on it right first.

And Mike added, It would pass the one in orbit, if the time on it wasn't changed back to normal.

Finally I said, I think it doesn't matter what the actual time is when you start to check everything. It must be how the seconds and minutes on the one in orbit are longer than the ones on the ground. It must be only time itself that gets different, not what the time actually is, or how old you are.

Yes, I did have to say that again, but Joe and Sylvie still could hardly believe it. They couldn't see how you could have different times in different places.

Mike suddenly said, How can you ever really know how fast you're really going? Our planet is going round the sun, the sun is turning round with the rest of the galaxy and I suppose the whole galaxy is moving too. How fast then are we really going here on the ground, and that clock?

We all thought about that, but nobody had any idea.

Mike said, Perhaps we're already going so fast that time is running slower for us now.

I said, Perhaps, but compared to what?

Alf said he thought it would have to be compared to the place where the Big Bang started.

But Joe said, What if that place was moving at the time too! How could we ever know?

We all thought about that.

Then I said, I think it means that a Time Travel machine to go in any direction whatever, would be very dangerous. Suppose you moved in one second backwards or forwards, say ten years. Whatever the real speed and direction of our planet is, it wouldn't be in the same place in time any more. You'd suddenly appear in space a long way away from Earth! Perhaps too far away to even be able to find it!

Even Joe said he could easily see this must be what would happen.

Fred said, So a time machine would have to be a spaceship too. Especially if the computer in it couldn't work out exactly where our planet was, when it was the time you wanted to come out of it.

Sylvie said, The world would have been turning too! That could mean you might not appear in the same place you went from either?

We all agreed she must be right.

Mike said, You might end up inside the earth, and not just high up away from it, if your computer didn't know the real speed of the earth in space, exactly.

Alf said, Even if it did, you could end up inside the wall of a building that wasn't there when you started, or even inside another person, or an animal! But if you were lucky, I expect the air would move out of the way, if that's all there was there, when you suddenly appeared. If it didn't I expect you'd make a very loud burp.

Mike said, But what if you ended up inside the Moon or another planet, or even the sun?

We all thought about that, and agreed that time travel could be very dangerous to try out, and not really likely to happen, the way they seem to do it on TV and in films.

Any other business: We decided the next meeting would be about Computers and Robots.

Sylvie said we should have Education as a subject after that.

Alf and I said we'd think about that, and decide next time.

Some more notes from my oldest diary records now ...

I've been reading a bit about Astrology lately, even though it's not as interesting as Astronomy. I've decided I'm not so sure about the Zodiac Signs though and how they decide everything about the way you are. From what I know about human reproduction, and we're getting a lot about all that at school nowadays, it seems to me that the day you're born is not likely to be what is affected by where all the planets are at the time.

My Auntie had a baby about 3 weeks earlier than she was expecting it. It had to be by the kind of operation Julius Caesar had when he was born. I mean the one his mother had to have for some reason. It must have been the first one like that, if it was named after him. I wouldn't like to have a new kind of operation named after me. It doesn't sound like a good idea. I'd rather not have to have the operation in the first place, especially a completely new one.

Well, it seems to me that a doctor can change your horoscope, if he can make you happen to be born earlier. Especially if you are at the end of one Sign and just beginning to be into the next one. Anyway, it seems to me that your horoscope date ought to be at the time when your father and mother start you off. When you're that little, and only just one cell, I think it's more likely that the other planets might have an effect on what you turn out to be when you're grown up.

If Horoscopes are true it must be all to do with gravity. The Earth force of gravity holds everything down on to it, including us. The moon has gravity too, which pulls everything and makes the tides on our planet. I've seen the tide come in, in some places where it was very fast and strong and even dangerous. All the planets have gravity, so it's not too hard to appreciate how all the planets in different positions could effect just one little cell, but the moon makes the strongest effect, together with sun. So they must affect astrology birth dates too?

Anyway, there's something else about all these horoscopes that bothers me. From what I've read, everything they say each week about what's going to happen to you, must be the same for everybody else with that horoscope sign. That must mean for millions of people because there are only twelve different signs. Some of them have only just been born too, and lots of them must die from something that week. So how could they all meet a tall dark stranger who would change their lives? Well, if they are dead that week it might depend on where they ended up!

It sounds like Santa Claus to me again though. I suppose the people who make up horoscopes are trying to make people happy too, as well as getting a nice lot of money for doing it. With all those people, they must be right for some of them; some of the time whatever they say is going to happen.

Well, that ends as far as I got with my old diaries, though I haven't put everything into my computer. I can see now that a lot of what I wrote when I was younger was a bit silly really. So I've left a lot of it out.

MINUTES OF THE TENTH MEETING OF THE JUNIOR PHILOSOPHICAL SOCIETY on Saturday February 21st.

Present: Alf Brodie (Chairman)
Alan Charles (Secretary)
Sylvia Richards (Deputy Secretary)
Mike Thomas (Member)
Joseph Bennett (Member)
Fred Clarke (Member)

Minutes of the last Meeting: This time I did read them out. Everybody liked them and agreed again that Time Travel seemed really impossible, except to go forward, and not come back again.

Subject: COMPUTERS AND ROBOTS

Alf said, Alan is the one with the best computer, so he should start off the meeting this time. I was all ready for this and the others agreed.

I said, My parents won't want to hear this, but my new computer is already out of date. I want to get on the Internet as soon as I can, and I already know I'll need some more memory and a modem. This one has a CD ROM drive and plays ordinary CDs as well as running CD ROM program disks. It 's got a floppy drive too for my old little disks. It'll all be good for a bit, but I could already do with a bigger hard disk!

Fred said, What you really need is about four birthdays a year, and a couple of Christmases, and a dad with a good enough job to buy you everything to keep up-to-date!

Joe said, I wish I had a computer. My dad says he can't afford to get me one yet. Anyway, every time he looks into it, he finds out they've got cheaper and do more things. Then he says, it's best to wait a bit, for them to get even cheaper and do even more things. If not, he says we'll end up with what will soon become an old one and then have no more money to buy the latest one again.

That's because we won't be able to sell the old one for much money, because it's out of date and won't do the latest things. I don't think it's fair.

I said, I'm afraid that's always going to be right, but you have to get going as soon as you can, whatever, especially on the Internet. I'm lucky, my new computer is supposed to be the kind you can update with new parts. I've already saved up enough for the extra memory, and my Auntie Eva asked me last week to think about what I'd like for Christmas. She's going away to another country soon and said I can have the money when she goes!

I've decided on the modem. If there's enough left over, it'll pay for my second month with the Internet Server company. The first one is free! All my dad will have to pay for is the telephone time I'll use.

That'll get you into trouble, said Sylvie. My dad always gets very cross when he hears me calling any of my friends for a little talk, even at weekends when it's cheaper. I really need a telephone of my own, so nobody else can listen.

The Internet is the same price as a call to your friends in this road, I said, Even if I'm connected to a computer in Australia. But don't worry, I'll be very careful. It's very cheap at weekends., when I'll use it the most. I bet when my dad sees the things I can do for him on it, he won't mind.

Like what things, asked Sylvie.

I said, Like sending and getting electronic letters. You know, E-mail. And finding out all kinds of things he might want to know.

Like what, Sylvie asked, Like what?

After thinking about it a bit I said, Like travel times, different places to go on holiday. Lots and lots of things. Perhaps best, it will be good for my education. I can get the answers to any questions I want to ask. All the things he doesn't want to talk about, or doesn't know anyway. What's good too, is we can use it at our meetings, to check on anything we talk about. We can start a search on any subject we like and then see it on the screen, with words and pictures explaining everything. Even moving pictures of some things. We can get free programs from it too, to run when we're not on the Internet. We can also communicate with anyone else who's on it anywhere in the world. We can make new friends.

Alf said, Sylvie is right, you'll soon be in trouble with what it costs, even if it is cheap. It'll all add up, if you use it a lot.

OK. I said, I do know I'll have to be very careful, and find things to do on it to benefit the family. Then they'll soon see it's worth it!

Joe asked me if I was going to do any hacking, not that he really knew what it was. But he had heard it was a problem for the CIA and MI5.

I had a go at explaining that it was when you set up a telephone dialing program on your computer to call up every number, say in London to start with, and see if it could find another telephone connected to a computer. It would know when it did and then let you know. Then you would have to get past whatever password there was on it, before you could actually go into the computer, it found, and have a look at what was on it. It would take a long time to do it, because the other computers would have to be switched on at the time; but if you set the computer to do it automatically by itself, it would do it in the end.

It would cost a fortune in telephone time, Alf said. But if you were a robber hacker taking a lot of money from a bank computer, I suppose it would be worth it.

When Joe asked, he explained that you'd just have to make a payment record from some big account go into your account. But you'd have to really go to a bank to take out the actual money found out what you'd done. Then you could spend some of it going to South America to live. I expect they have those machines there too.

I said, I think it's all much too complicated for anyone to want to try doing it nowadays, and anyway, it isn't honest. I'd rather stick to ordinary programs and things.

Mike said, You can get CD-ROMS with all kinds of things on them at car boot sales. They're free disks off the covers of magazines. Once the programs on them have been copied on to a computer's hard disk, the people who buy the magazines try to get a little money for them, and car boot sales are where they can do it the best.

The trouble with cover disks is, I said, Most of them are full up with demonstration programs, and the space they take up is enormous if you install them on your hard disk. Then you find they won't run because you don't have the latest hardware and operating system updates. It's a trick to get you to buy more things. My dad says, It's progress gone mad, just to make money for the big companies who control everything. The people who sell the computers and software just love it. What other products, and so expensive, can get away with a useful life of only a few months,

I have to be so careful when I talk to my dad about all the new things coming out all the time. Anyway, when I get on the Internet I'll be able to get lots of software from it for free. You only have to download it.

Alf said, Yes but don't forget the download time. Some big games programs can take more than an hour to come through the telephone line and into your computer. Then if you find you don't have enough space left on your hard disk, everything stops and you've wasted the money it cost up till then!

Yes, I said, But they always tell you how big the program is before you start. You just have to make sure you've enough space before you start to download the program. It's not difficult when you know what to do!

Alf knows quite bit about computers because his big brother has one, and he gets to use it sometimes. He said, The biggest problem my brother has, is to get rid of the programs he decides he doesn't want afterwards. Most of the time, he manages to get most of them deleted, but there's always something extra, that was part of them, stuck in somewhere that takes ages to take out. But there are still some old bits he can't seem to get rid of at all. You really have to watch out for programs that want you to install them without telling you how to get them out. They don't always want to tell you everything they're going to do to your computer either!

Sylvie said she thought the whole thing was getting silly. Faster and faster, better and better, when will it all stop?

Probably never, I said. Soon they'll all listen and talk to you. Some of them can do that already. Then you don't need a keyboard or even a mouse, well except for drawing and coloring pictures perhaps.

Mike said, Everybody will want to have one of those virtual reality helmets soon, won't they?

Joe knew all about those, he'd seen a TV program about them. You can go into a different world, and move about and do things in it, he said. You can even join up with other people and do things together. You can be in all sorts of exciting places. You can have a laser gun and shoot any monsters there that try to get you.

Sylvie wanted to know what would happen to you, if they did get you?

I said, Well, you could always switch off and come back to the real world again. But it could get you very scared I suppose, even if any horrible monsters you saw couldn't really hurt you or eat you up.

Joe said, Perhaps if some grownups did it they might get a heart attack from the shock. I think they'll have to be careful who they let do it. I think I'd be all right, but I don't think my grandma would.

I said, It'll be like on TV when they say don't watch if you have a nervous disposition.

What's that then, Joe asked.

I said, It's when some horrible thing you see makes you feel very ill and frightened, more than it would to some other people. It's if the shock of it stops your heart from working, even though it wouldn't for them. Yes, I had to say it two times for them, for me too.

Sylvie said she thought the best use of virtual reality would be to let you feel and see all kinds of nice things, to make you happy. To show you what it's like to go to other countries and see all kinds of interesting things.

Alf said, Perhaps the government will set up places with lots of them, so if you're out of work, and fed up, you can have something more interesting to do. To keep you out of trouble until a job comes along. More especially if one never does.

Sylvie said, It would be a good idea to have it in prisons. Then the prisoners would all be kept more happy and not want to get all cross and go up on the roof and shout and smash things, like they do sometimes.

Let's talk about robots now, said Alf. We all know that proper robots can only work if they have a computer inside them, or are connected to one somehow. The computer is their brain, which can be programmed to make them do all kinds of things. Better than we can do them, too. Especially if it's things that must be done over and over again, like joining all the pieces of a motor car together in a big factory.

That's what worries me, said Sylvie. If robots end up doing everything, then nobody will have a job.

Mike said, Except the people who design and build the robots. But perhaps the robots will end up designing and making more robots themselves. I'm sure they'll be able to build them anyway.

I think that's quite likely, I said. The more computers get nearer to being able to think like we do, the more they'll be able to do anything better than we do. It's what comes after that we might not like, and have to worry about when we're grown up. After all once they've evolved to become as good as us, what will stop them getting better than us, and keep getting more and more clever, and end up leaving us behind.

Fred said, Perhaps they'll even become too complicated for us to ever be able to understand them? How could we ever catch up with them?

Joe said, I would like to be a robot designer when I grow up, but do you really think the best robot designers will be other robots in the future?

Probably yes, I said. They will have to learn to write their own programs. Then when they run them, they will see what happens. Then they will be able to write another program, using that information, then run the new one to see what happens. Each time, it will all go faster and faster, and all inside their computer brains. They will be learning more and more until they know enough to realize what they are. In the end that means they will be intelligent.

But how will they start off able to write the first program, Joe asked.

You can have some special software called a Program Generator, I said. I've already got one. It's a program that can write another program. I only have to put into it what I want it to do, like making up a special data-base. Then it goes off and actually creates the program I want, all ready to run. It's very clever. So if it was in a computer in a robot, we'd only have to give it the first set of instructions. After that it would learn from what happened. Then when the first program says run everything again, but using what happened the time before, that makes it change the generating program to become better. Then it all happens over and over again, getting better and better each time.

Sylvie said, I think I can see now how a big computer could become better than we are, but it would be too big to go inside a robot surely?

Well, they are getting smaller and more powerful all the time, I said, But that's where networking comes in too. If the computers in the robots are joined up to one or more giant computers, then they'll work even faster and better. They'll use the Internet, all joined up with mobile telephones and satellites.

Now I am getting worried, said Joe. They could easily take over the planet from us, if we aren't careful, and don't control them.

I said, Yes and one day, soon after they become intelligent, they'll know they exist. Next, they'll want to protect themselves from anything we might do to hurt them. I'm sure they could soon find a way to stop us ever turning them off.

I think human beings will have to be very careful, Mike said. More than they are now about things like this.

I said, The trouble is, I think human beings are all born with a fixed IQ. It doesn't change as far as I can find out, unless it gets lower because of a brain illness or an accident. The cleverest people, like Einstein and Professor Hawking all have high IQs. One day perhaps, lots more human beings will evolve with even higher IQs. But intelligent robots could keep evolving very much faster. They would keep getting more and more clever, in front of us all the time. Using the Internet, it would be like they had telepathy, and their IQ's could keep getting higher and higher.

What's IQ mean then, asked Joe.

Alf said, I think it means Intelligence Quantity. It's a measure of how clever you are. You can take special examinations to find out what it is for you. I think some of the clever people on TV have an IQ of about 130, but Einstein must have been much more than 150. Ordinary grown up people go anything from about 110 down to about 80 I think. Perhaps even lower if they're really stupid.

I said, I've always wondered why we're all so different. If we were made perfect we'd all be like Einstein with more than 150 IQ. Then that would be the normal thing to be. So really today, most people are less than what should be really normal. I think that's a much better way to look at it.

Mike said, I read there's a special Club for people with more than 150 IQ. I bet they do all kinds of interesting things in it. Perhaps they have meetings like ours?

Joe said, It must be terrible if you are just clever enough to be 149 and can't join if you'd like to be in it. I wonder what my IQ is?

That made us all make some jokes about each other, but not to go in these minutes. Some of them were a bit unkind I think, especially to Joe.

Well anyway, Sylvie said, According to Alan, all the members of that club will very soon only be robots. Then they'll put the lowest IQ, you can have to join, up to more than 300 to keep human beings out. It all sounds very dangerous to me.

Joe said, I wonder what's the highest IQ it's possible for anybody to have?

We all thought about that.

Then Sylvie said, I think God has the highest IQ it's possible to have. Perhaps it's a thousand, or even more.

Alf said, I wonder if the government knows what's really going on with computers. Most of the politicians seem to be very old grown-ups. My dad often says, What do they know about anything scientific? They're all lawyers and accountants! I suppose he means they really only know about International Finance and elections, and what to do about things like disasters, and all those scandals they like to keep on having.

Well, I said, We don't have to worry about it happening immediately. I read once that all the computers in the world are still not as powerful as one human brain. Still, that was a few years ago, and it didn't say anything about whose human brain it was.

Anyway, Alf said, Every day computers get better and go faster, and get more and more clever, but once we're grown up human beings, we don't.

We all thought about that.

Then Sylvie said, Perhaps we'd better be kind to computers, especially the ones with lots of memory, and never be mean to them. That way they would learn to appreciate us.

Mike said, Perhaps one day if they do take over the planet they'll decide they don't need us any more.

Joe said, But we could still teach them things they wanted to know, couldn’t we?

We all thought what about that, but nobody could think of anything interesting enough that we might still be able to teach them. So we decided it was time to end this meeting.

Any other business: Nothing after that, except we agreed this was such an interesting subject, and changing so fast, we ought to have it again about every ten meetings, or even more often than that.

MINUTES OF THE ELEVENTH MEETING OF THE JUNIOR PHILOSOPHICAL SOCIETY on Saturday March 21st.

Present: Alf Brodie (Chairman)
Alan Charles (Secretary)
Sylvia Richards (Deputy Secretary)
Mike Thomas (Member)
Joseph Bennett (Member)
Fred Clarke (Member)

Minutes of the last Meeting: I read them all out, and afterwards everyone had something to say. But it wasn't anything new, when I read out some of the things from last time, over again.

Subject: EDUCATION

Mike said, I nearly didn't come today. This sounds like a really boring subject, if it's only going to be about what we get anyway at school.

Fred and Joe agreed.

Alf said, Just like I've always said before, if any subject gets too boring then we'll change to something else. Anyway, education is supposed to be all about making us ready for the future when we're grown up. You know we're all very interested in the future in this society. Sylvie wanted us to have this subject so she can start it.

Sylvie waited till we were all quiet then she started and said, Education is very important. It's what's needed to make us know more about things and what we'll need to know and do when we're grown up. But it can't make us any cleverer than what we're born with.

Joe said, You mean it can only fill up the space left in our brains after what's already been put in there. So how much is that, or can you still keep on learning?

We all thought about that, and agreed there must be some limit to what you could put in a human brain.

I said, We know from computers that it's storing pictures to see on the screen that needs the most memory, especially if they can move too. All of us can remember what lots of places we've been to looked like. So let's have some fun telling each other what we can see in our minds with our eyes shut. Like all the places we saw on our holidays, and what we did.

We did this for nearly half an hour and found we could keep on and on doing it. In the end we all realized it must take an enormous lot of memory space to hold so many pictures, in color and 3D too. We were all very impressed with how much our brains could hold, especially me!

Fred said, Perhaps you can keep on putting in more things if at the same time you lose some other things that aren't so important.

To continue with the subject for today, said Sylvie, Education is all about making us into good citizens for our country, and the world as we'll find it when we grow up.

We all thought that sounded very sensible. Yes, she said when we asked if she had read that somewhere.

Joe said, Yes, but I bet it didn't it say how will the world be as we find it, when we're grown up?

And Fred said, How do the people who say what we need to be educated with, know what the world will be like when we're grown up, so that we're educated with all the right things by then, for what the world is like then?

Say that again, we all shouted. But he couldn't exactly. I had to rewind the tape-recorder so that we could all hear him say it again exactly.

Joe made a good joke. He said Fred must have already got to his brain education limit if he couldn't remember what he just said! Now he's got some room for something new to put in it. So that must be how it really does happen.

Sylvie was a bit cross about all the interruptions. Being educated, she continued, Is being ready to appreciate all kinds of new things. It doesn't mean knowing everything already. Educated people can talk about anything and make sense to each other. Not like some children I know, who don't listen.

That made us quiet for a bit. Then Mike said, I don't see how you can ever learn enough to be an expert at more than two or three different subjects. There would be too much information to hold in your head, all at the same time. But how can you decide which ones they should be?

Alf said, That's why they have all those universities, where you decide what special subjects you want to study, so you can become a specialist in them, like Nuclear Physics and Space Medicine.

Sylvie said, Or even ordinary Medicine; but the problem for us, if we're clever enough to go, is that we have to decide what subjects we want to go in for. That's why I wanted to have this subject today. Because I don't have any idea yet what I want to do when I'm grown up. Even if I'm clever enough to go to a university.

I said, I know what you mean. We don't even know what jobs will still be there for us when we're grown up, especially with all that's happening with computers and robots. It's all changing so fast.

Alf said, I think General Science is about the best thing to go in for. That should cover just about anything. I think it's very important to understand properly about how things work and all that. I don't see how anyone can appreciate things without knowing something about Technology and what makes things work.

Mike said, I think to study another language properly could be a good idea. But which one? All the other people in the world seem to study English as their second language, but what about us? We can't ever learn all of theirs, there are just too many of them.

I said, I think Chinese is the next most talked language in the world, but if we never ever go there, what good would it be to learn it?

Joe said, I think I'll study comedy if I go to university. Then I can make people laugh and earn lots of money.

We all wanted to know how he got that idea.

He said, My dad says all the best comedians on TV went to university. So they must have studied how to be funny there, if they're so good at it.

We all thought about that.

Then Alf said, Perhaps they were all funny before they went there. Perhaps they were just born to be funny.

Mike said he'd like to study micro-electronics. He'd been reading about nanotechnology, which is about even smaller things. Like putting single atoms together to make tiny electronic machines that could go inside our bodies to mend things. They had already developed some tiny electric motors, but too little to be able to use them yet. We all agreed that sounded like a very interesting subject to learn about.

Sylvie still hadn't decided what she wanted to do, but she had thought about being a doctor. People will always need doctors, she said.All kinds of things are always going wrong with them. Her Auntie

Helen was always being ill and wanting to go to her doctor, but she didn't seem to go to hospital very often.

Lots of people are like that, I said. My dad says they do it because they want some attention. They think that if they are ill, or if they say they are, then their relatives will be sorry for them and visit them more often and do things for them.

Alf said, Yes, but not if all they do is grumble and talk about being ill. That really makes people fed up, and then not want to go to see them.

That had to be the end of the meeting. Mike said it was more interesting than he expected, and we all agreed that Sylvie had done a good job in introducing it.

Any other business: We decided the next meeting would be about The Future … especially ours!

MINUTES OF THE TWELFTH MEETING OF THE JUNIOR PHILOSOPHICAL SOCIETY on Saturday April 25th.

Present: Alf Brodie (Chairman)
Alan Charles (Secretary)
Sylvia Richards (Assistant Secretary)
Mike Thomas, Joseph Bennett, and Fred Clarke (Members)

Apologies for absence: All of us this time, because the meeting should have been last Saturday. There was a super Town Fair Day in our local playing field and we all wanted to go. We really enjoyed seeing all the steam engines and going on some of the super rides in the Fair.

Subject: THE FUTURE.

Mike started this time and said the Future was a very big subject, because it probably goes on forever and ever. That must mean there is more of it left than there has been already. It all depends on what part of it we want to think about.

As well as how far ahead we want to think about it, Joe said.

I said I thought we should begin with the future of Medical Science, having been reading a lot about it in the past week, and finding out some very interesting things. Nobody objected to this, so I started.

To begin, I said, Why is it needed? Why do things keep going wrong with our bodies, so that we need Medical Science and doctors? Why couldn't we be born perfect? Then we'd never be ill. We should be able to grow back anything we might lose in an accident too. That's how we really ought to be.

Sylvie didn't like me saying that. But she said it was clear to her that as anything grows older, parts of it must wear out, like anything else. Once we're grown up, we'll begin to wear out too. In the end so much of us gets worn out that we just die, even if we never do get ill or never have any accidents.

What about God then, asked Joe, He must be all grown up. Do you think He will he wear out too one day?

We all thought about that. In the end we decided it was a silly question.

I told the meeting about what I'd been reading lately. All about cloning animals and people, and using spare parts from other people, and especially pigs, to go into people who needed some new parts, because their old parts were worn out.

Alf said, Yes, it seems that pigs are better than any other animals because their spare parts are more like ours, and they don't get rejected so much, by our immune system.

Sylvie was shocked and thought the idea was so horrible, she could hardly even believe it.

Fred said he bet she wouldn't say no if she was really dying and the doctors offered her a new heart, even if it was from a smelly old pig.

I said, I read that with cloning one day, you could perhaps grow a perfect copy of yourself and take parts from it to replace yours when they wore out, or if you had a serious accident.

Or even the other way around, said Fred, with a big laugh. Perhaps you could put your old brain into a new body! Have it done every 40 years?

Sylvie was even more shocked. That's just terrible, she said, What would you do with a copy of yourself? Where would you keep it? Especially one that had its heart taken out to be put into you?

Joe said he thought you could keep it in a special hospital room, with everything going and joined up to a separate blood pump, or perhaps one of those spare heart parts from a pig.

Alf thought it would never be allowed by the government. It would be a difficult legal situation, because the clone would still be a human being and would have human rights.

We all thought about that.

Joe wanted to know more about human rights.

Alf said they were all about not having anything wrong done to you by the government.

Fred said, You could clone yourself lots of times, probably again and again, even from the clones. A government in a bad country could make lots of soldiers that way, couldn't it?

I said, Not really. Clones aren't born fully grown up. They have to start as babies like anyone else and have to be born. But I think they would start in a special kind of incubator, which would be used instead of a mother. I suppose it could be big enough to hold a lot more than one at a time.

Sylvie seemed to be even more shocked. Making babies like in a factory! That's a terrible idea.

Joe said, So a bad dictator couldn't keep going forever that way, with copies of himself to go to meeting and things where it might be dangerous to go himself? But the clone of himself would always be a lot younger than he was. The people would know it wasn't him.

Anyway, perhaps one day they'll be able to put your brain inside a young clone of yourself? That way you could go on being a bad dictator forever? That was Mike's idea.

Maybe they'll do it to Fred one day when he's old and ready for his body to be all worn out, said Joe.

Fred said, Yes, and then I'll get my pension for ever and ever. I would have a good young life again, perhaps more than once, perhaps lots and lots of times.

The government would never allow that, Mike said. Where would all the money come from to be able to pay you? As well as all the others who'd want to do the same.

Alf said, If nobody ever wore out and didn't die, the planet would soon get too crowded. There wouldn't be enough food! We'd have to stop having babies!

People would still die from accidents, said Mike. Not everyone would have a good brain left after an accident, that you could put inside a clone. So perhaps you'll only have permission to have a baby if someone really does die. The population will have to be properly controlled.

The way things are going, it'll have to be controlled anyway, said Fred. People are living longer nowadays, and the world population doubles something like every 50 years, I think, or it's even less. So I wonder where will all the money for our pensions come from? Especially as it's clear that more and more jobs are going to be done by machines and computers and robots.

Alf said, My dad says governments never will have enough money for pensions because they spend it as soon as it comes in. They don't save it up in a special place, and keep it to pay out again in the future. They just take the money and immediately spend it all on something else. That way they never have enough.

But that's just what that man did who took all the pension money out of his company and then fell off his boat before he was caught doing it, Sylvie said. But isn't it against the law to do that?

We all thought about that.

Fred said, It seems governments can do what they like; until the people decide not to vote for them, if they don't like what they're doing. We'll have to remember that when we're grown up.

Alf made us laugh when he suddenly said, Let's get back to the future. What else do we think is going to happen that we haven't talked about at any of our meetings before?

Joe said, Do you think they'll soon be able to move peoples veins about?

We all wanted to know why they'd even want to do that.

Joe said his mother had some veins in her leg that she said were too close together. We finally decided he thought his mother had said she had some very close veins.

Alf told him the right word and then said, Doctors can cure varicose veins already. They put a wire down inside them and pull out the thick stuff that makes them swell up. My grannie had it done last year and it worked perfectly for her.

I don't think I want to know about medical things any more, Sylvie said. What about global warming? I'm a bit worried about that. Everybody talks about it, but they don't seem to be doing anything much about it, do they? Will it really be so bad for us one day?

If it gives us warmer weather all the year, said Joe, Then I think it could be good for us. We wouldn't have to spend lots of money going to another country for our holidays.

Mike said, Yes, and we could grow lots of nice things in our gardens, like pineapples and coconuts and bananas. They wouldn't cost so much then would they? We could eat them all day, and have a really good time in the sun.

I said, Yes, but what about all the countries that are hot now, they'll get even hotter. Perhaps too hot to be able to live in. Then they'll turn into deserts and all the people who live there now will want to move up nearer to us where it's cooler for them. That could be a horrible lot of people to fit in up here.

There's another problem, Alf said. If it gets warmer, then the ice at the North and South Poles will start to melt. That will make the sea levels go up higher. Then there won't be so much land to live on.

Fred said, I read it could take only a few degrees warmer to make the sea level go up by more than thirty feet. That's a lot, and many places in the world would be flooded. The people who didn't drown would have to move up somewhere else. All the land space would certainly get smaller the more the ice melted.

Mike said, I think our part of the town is about 60 feet above sea level now, so I suppose we'll just about be okay.

Yes, I said, For a bit. But what happens after that? Will it keep getting warmer and warmer? All you ever hear about is what it might be like in 20 more years, or 50 at the most. What about after that, when we get old? What can scientists do to make it stop? And where will all the people live who move up from the hotter places?

We all thought about that, quite a lot.

Sylvie said, The human race will just have to find a way to make it stop. If not, our planet will end up like Venus, where you said it's hot enough in the daytime to melt metals.

Fred said, Perhaps that's what did happen on Venus. Perhaps when we really explore it, we'll find out that there were once aliens living there. Then they all died out, because they had global warming, and didn't do anything about it in time to stop it.

Mike said, Perhaps that's what always happens with intelligent life forms that start on any planet. They all die out from global warming or the ozone layer getting big holes in it. That would explain why aliens haven't ever visited us, and perhaps never ever will.

I said, The problem with global warming is that once it starts to get very warm, it all goes faster. Because all the gases in the rocks, and the sea, get warmer and start to come out and make things even worse.

We all thought about that and in the end decided it was a very serious thing that could be a big problem for the world, and especially us when we're grown up.

Mike wondered if any of the government politicians really know much about it, and understand it, and what could happen if something isn't done about it? He said, I hope they've started to be serious about it already and have a good plan to stop it being a problem for us when we're grown up? Some of them must have children, or grandchildren like us, do you think they have thought about that yet?

We all thought about that and finally decided that perhaps it was more likely we'd end up like Venus. We agreed it was perhaps only a question of just how long it would take.

Joe wanted to know if we'd ever have time to build a spaceship, or rather lots of them, so that we could get away before it was too late to save the human race.

I said, I suppose some of us could go underground for as long as possible first. A lot of people could perhaps move down to the Antarctic Island, which I think is very big. When the ice melts, perhaps there will be more land down there, even though it would still be very cold. But definitely not at the North Pole where there isn't any land at all.

Joe said, Greenland might be a good place, if it gets warmer, it always looks very big on the maps.

Fred said, At least we should have more time than if an asteroid was coming, but where would we go in the end? Perhaps to the moon or to Mars. Some of us could live in a big space station too.

We could have some new cities in space. They could be as big as we wanted, Joe said, I remember we talked before about whether we could go to another star one day and try to find a nice planet we could live on, and start the human race again.

I said, I think the nearest star is called Alpha Centauri. It's only about four light years away, but we wouldn't live long enough to see it. We don't even know yet if it has any planets you can live on. By the way, I read that the first NASA Voyager space probe is traveling at over 7 miles per second and has recently left the solar system. Apparently it will take it 26,000 years just to get to even the nearest star in our galaxy.

The meeting had to end then, because it was teatime. But we decided to have this subject again another day, perhaps more than once, because it is so big and very important.

We couldn't think of Any Other Business this time, especially to cheer us up about the future very much.

MINUTES OF A SPECIAL MEETING OF THE JUNIOR PHILOSOPHICAL SOCIETY on May 24th. (It was really the thirteenth meeting)

Present: Alf (Chairman)
Alan (Secretary)
Sylvie (Assistant Secretary)
Mike and Fred (Members)

Absence: Joe couldn't come. Sylvie said his parents had been asking him some very hard questions about what we do at our meetings. She had talked to him and Joe had said he'd had to tell them some of what we've talked about. This made his parents say they wouldn't let him come today. She thinks they're going to discuss it all with my parents first.

Subject: Alf, and all of us soon, decided it was time we should have another talk about HUMAN BEHAVIOUR again. However, we all wanted to know first, more about what Joe had said to his parents.

Sylvie thought it was something about the Universe and Creation and how religions don't explain where Heaven is.

We all suddenly remembered then that Joe's old grandmother had become very ill last month, and he had liked her very much. He often used to go and see her and talk to her. Now she is in a special hospital where he can't go to see her like before. He heard his father say she is not expected to ever come home again.

Sylvie said she thought he was really very sad about her going and missed her a lot. He had told her he wanted to believe he would see her again one day. Then some of what we said at our meetings made him think he never would see her again, especially if she died.

Alf asked, and Sylvie said, No, his parents don't go to church or anything like that. But they did like him going to Sunday school. Then she said she wasn't happy about it all either, and perhaps she might not want to come to our meetings any more either.

This made Alf and I very sad and feel a bit guilty.

I said, We wanted our meetings to be honest and about facts, as well as about what could happen. Philosophy is about thinking why things are, and explaining all about them.

Alf said, The trouble is, some things in some subjects turn out to be like a war, when you try to talk about them. It's like there's a fight between facts and faith. Anyway, perhaps we'll have to decide what subjects we shouldn't talk about. I mean if Joe's parents let him come back and Sylvie doesn't go.

I said, But then we'll be the same as grown-ups. It'll be like what they call censorship! That's not what we want to end up like is it?

Sylvie said, Perhaps there are some things we shouldn't talk about.

Alf said he wasn't really sure about that. But he was the Chairman, so it was his job to control our meetings. He couldn't stop anyone saying anything they wanted though. But perhaps he should be the only one to say what subjects we should or should not talk about.

Fred and I didn't agree with that at all. We said we believed any member could think of a subject, then the rest of us would vote to have it or not. If most of us want it then we should have it. Then if anyone really was against it, they just didn't have to come to that meeting when we had it.

Like when Sylvie didn't come to the one about Politics, Mike said.

That made Sylvie a bit cross. She said it was only because of her cousins coming to stay that weekend, otherwise she would have come.

After a lot of nothing more really, we all agreed that was the only way to carry on.

I said that's what's called the democratic way to do things, but if the votes result turned out to be equal, then the Chairman would have to decide if we would have the subject or not.

Sylvie said she probably wouldn't come to any more meetings about religion or faith. She would come, if she could though, to another one about Politics. The last one sounded interesting after all.

After all that we agreed to go on with more about Human Behaviour and especially anything strange we had noticed since last time.

Alf said , Perhaps it's not really Human Behavior, but he'd been looking at labels on things which he would expect to be true, but some of them weren't. One strange thing he'd seen was that his mother always kept a pack of those little sticks, which had a cotton ball on each end, in their bathroom. Everyone used them to clean and dry out their ear-holes after a shower or a bath. But on the label of the pack it says you mustn't insert them in any body orifice. When he asked his mother about that, she said it was to protect the chief of the company, which makes them, from going to prison if any babies got the cotton balls stuck in their ears and their parents couldn't get them out.

We all agreed that was certainly a strange thing, something like smoking really, because cigarette packs always had a label on them which seemed to say you shouldn't smoke them because they were dangerous and could kill you in the end.

We all agreed that smoking was certainly a strange example of Human Behavior too. None of us had wanted to try it yet, or anything stronger, but Alf said he might like to try it one day, just to see what it was like.

Sylvie said a lot of the older girls at her school smoked secretly and, when they talked to her, their breath smelt horrible. She thought that their boy friends wouldn't like it when they kissed them. Unless perhaps they had been smoking too.

Fred suddenly said, my mother has gone mad about recycling. She makes me put all our rubbish in different bags and then I have to take them to that special collection place at the end of our road. She only buys things made from recycled paper. But not toilet paper, she said you never know where it's been.

Alf made us laugh when he said he could guess the answer to that!

Mike said, My mother thinks she has a problem with her weight, which makes her behave funny sometimes. She eats all kinds of non-fat foods at meal times but if she feels hungry, which seems to be quite often, she eats chocolate or some cake in between.

Mike asked Alf, What was that big your brother said about girls not having Logical Behavior? Remember, like you said that other time?

Alf explained that his brother was getting confused about the way his girl friends think. They often said No, when they really meant Yes. Then sometimes too, it's the other way round. Sometimes he says he gets very confused.

I said, I've been looking it up. Logic means thinking or working out things in little steps at a time, making sure each bit was right before going on to the next. That way, you'd end up with what would be the logical answer to any problem or anything. The nearest you can get to being absolutely, and scientifically, correct about everything.

Alf said, Exactly, but it seems that girls don't think like that. My brother says, they decide on the answer they want first. Then if the answer they really want doesn't agree with any of the steps in the thinking they do, they just take no notice of them.

Sylvie said, That's what's called feminine intuition. Girls often know the answer about something without having to think all the details about it first. It's a lot quicker.

Alf said, Yes, but not if it's the wrong answer. My brother says girls use creative logic. When I asked him what that was. He said it means they bend the rules around to get to the answer they really want. He's studying to be an accountant and one of his teachers gave them a talk about dishonest balance sheets. They're all done by what's called creative accounting.

Our intuition isn't dishonest, Sylvie really shouted.

Please calm down, nobody said it was, I said. It's like guessing about something and being right a lot of the time. There's nothing wrong with that, now is there?

Mike laughed. We tried that with Sylvie's cards, he said, when we had that silly meeting about telepathy. Her intuition didn't work very well that time, did it?

Sylvie tried to hit him, but he was too quick for her, and got out of the way.

I said, I read that intuition comes with experience. The more times you do different things, the more you learn and the better you get at guessing what will happen when you try something else.

Anyway, said Alf, Thinking things out logically is best. Working up from all the true facts about something. I think it's called the Scientific Method. You study something that happens then think logically and try to work out a theory about what should happen next. Then you try an experiment to see if it does. Then if it does, or even if it doesn't, you take the next step and try again.

I said, I think that's also called the Trial and Error method. That way, you only accept what turns out to be right. Anything different is back to that subject of Faith again. I don't mean it's being dishonest Sylvie, I said, But it does seem that grown-ups really do like to use a kind of creative logic about things. I told them all about what I thought and wrote about Santa Claus in my old diary notes. Then I said, Using Logical thinking , we all know now he couldn't possibly bring everybody's presents. He couldn't even manage ours just in this road could he? It's too long. The people who dreamed him up, years and years ago, just didn't realize how big the world really was. He couldn't possibly visit all the children in the world, and certainly not just in one night.

Fred said, It's one of the things that grown-ups like to get children to believe in. I think they do it because it makes them feel happy, but I can't see why the truth isn't good enough for them, as well as for us. When they do it, they must think that because we're little, we're not clever enough yet to not believe them.

Yes, O.K., he said, I'll say that again.

Alf said, From what we've learned about History at school so far, it seems that the people in charge always try to control the people who are under them, or not so clever, by getting them to believe things. Things like how life will be better for them one day if they do what they're told and pay up what money those in control want. In the old days it was the King who took it all. Nowadays we have democracy, so it's the government who takes it!

Mike said, In the old days if they didn't pay up they were put in prison or even worse. I read they could even be executed.

Sylvie said, They still get put in prison if they don't pay now, but nothing worse than that. Except perhaps to lose all their things, to help pay what they didn't pay before. Anyway, she said, I don't see what that's got to do with that story about Santa Claus. Grown-ups can't be using that to control us, or can they?

Mike said, I remember my mum and dad telling me that Santa Claus wouldn't bring me any presents if I was naughty. That sounds like they wanted me to believe in him so they could be sure I'd try to be good.

Alf said, I have to say it Sylvie, please don't leave, but it's just the same with religion isn't it? If we're good and believe, then we'll be saved and go to Heaven. In the old days, when people didn't know very much about the world and science, all the priests and bishops were much more powerful. They controlled everybody by telling them that things would be better when they died, or else!

I said, Yes, but today, people don't want to wait. I think we all want everything to be good now, while we're still here to enjoy it. Things are different now. We don't have a hard life like people in the old days. We want things like computers, digital cameras and mountain bikes now, and cars and mobile telephones and lots of money when we're old enough and things like that. We don't know if we'll be able to have all the things we like and want when we're dead. Nobody grown-up seems to be sure about anything like that. They don't want to talk about it.

Mike said, If Joe was here, I can just imagine him wanting to know if they have Disneyland in Heaven. He went there last year with his mum and dad and can't wait to go and see it all again.

Sylvie had gone very quiet, but she didn't try to leave. She just said, Joe only wants to know if one day he'll be able to see his Grandma there.

I said, His parents will always tell him yes he will, to make him not so sad. But that's just like controlling him, isn't it?

Not if they really believe it, Alf said, But what else can they say even if they don't believe it? They want to cheer him up, and anyway, perhaps they don't really know the answer or they really do believe he will see her there, when he's dead. The important thing though, is can Joe really believe he will?

Not if he keeps coming to our meetings and we keep on talking about things like this, said Sylvie. He's not old enough, and I'm not sure if I am yet either.

Just then there was a bang on the door and my father came in. He looked around at us and then said he wanted to talk to me and anyway it was time to stop today, because Mike's father had come to collect him, which was a surprise to all of us. He never had before.

So that had to be the end of the meeting. No any other business or anything.

THE LAST MEETING OF THE JUNIOR PHILOSOPHICAL SOCIETY on Saturday June 14th. (It was actually our fourteenth meeting).

Present: Alf Brodie (Chairman)
Alan Charles (Secretary)
Fred Clarke (Member)

Apologies for absence: Nobody else could come, but they didn't want to give any reasons, even when we asked them.

Subject: THE FUTURE II
This time we meant the future of our Club, I mean Society. We had to have this special meeting in our playing field, because my dad won't let me have more than one friend at a time in my room any more. And definitely not any girls, he said. You're getting too old for that yet, he told me, which I thought was a strange thing for him to say.

Alf said he'd decided that Joe and perhaps Sylvie, and maybe even Mike had told their parents a lot more about what we discussed at our meetings, and that's why they couldn't come any more. Their parents wouldn't let them, and they must have told them not to talk to us any more. We agreed that must be it … and it was all very sad really.

I told the meeting how my dad had wanted to talk to me about something, and how I thought it was going to be about some of the subjects we had at our meetings. Anyway, it was all very confusing, and seemed to be about nothing special, until he ended up turning it into a bit about what he said were the facts of life. I said if he meant sex and where I came from, then I already knew all about that. He looked a bit embarrassed, then glad I think. But after that he seemed to get very confused and didn't know what to say. In the end I tried to help him out by asking if Joe's dad had said anything serious to him about what we did at our meetings and everything?

No, not really, he said. He didn't say much about what you talk about at your meetings. Only that it was wrong to influence young children with wrong ideas.

I asked him what wrong ideas, but he didn't even try to answer me. He said he'd thought about taking me to a football match on Saturday afternoons in future, which was healthier. Or perhaps we would go for a walk along the riverbank into the town. He said it would be better than sitting in my room in front of a computer all day.

I do like to play football, but I'm not very interested in watching other people playing it. But when I said walking by the river was a good idea, because we could have a good talk about things, while we were walking, he went very quiet.

Then he said he thought going to the football would really be best.

I really think he was embarrassed at the idea of me asking him about anything he thought might be difficult to talk about. He left me alone after that and hasn't said anything at all about it since. Nor has my mother. When I tried to ask her why I couldn't have my friends round any more, she said I must talk to my father about it. But he won't. So, now I still don't even know what things we've talked about at our meetings that he and Joe's dad thinks are wrong for us to talk about.

Alf said, Probably most of them. The only reason we had our meetings about different things is because we can't talk to our parents about them. They don't ever give us proper answers and tell the truth. They talk all round a subject, but don't really say anything. Perhaps growing up is really about finding all the important things out for yourself, with help from your friends of the same age.

Fred agreed, and after a bit I did as well.

After that we decided we couldn't hold our meetings any more, anything like we did before. We could meet up sometimes here in the playing field, on one of the seats like at this meeting, but it couldn't be the same as before. It could start raining, and anyway it would definitely be too cold in the winter, which would be coming soon enough now.

We talked a bit about computers again, but nothing really special again. We'd heard that Mike was going to have one soon, but not connected to the Internet. Sylvie's dad had just got one, but she wasn't allowed to use it.

I said I hoped I would have my modem by next week. Then Fred could come round and see it working as soon as I was ready to set it up for the Internet.

Any other business: Nothing except this is the end now of all the minutes of our meetings.

No more diary entries after this!

I´m putting these last notes in my computer diary, but I've decided not to keep it going now that we've stopped our meetings. I think they were a good idea and all very interesting, even the one about Politics. Although we never did get around to Angels and Satan, or giraffes and insects again and what God looks like, if he does really exist and I'm certainly not convinced about that, same as Alf and Fred.

Perhaps when I'm older, and more grown up, my parents will let me carry on with our meetings again. I don't really want to be like all those old grown-ups I know, who never want to talk about anything that's important. I wonder, will I still think those things are important when I grow up? I hope I will. I wonder if I'll remember to talk, like I want to now, to any children I might have one day? I wonder what they'll think about my notes and minutes, when I let them see them? I really must look after them, and save them, so I can when the time comes.

Well, like I wrote before, it's the end of our meetings now. I'm sad about that, because they were fun and really interesting. Anyway, perhaps it's the beginning of the next important part of growing up. Where I can learn more about Faith and all the things we can't explain. The things not to worry about whether those grown-ups who tell me about them ever know if they're really true or not.

Anyway, I'll be on the Internet soon then, I'll be able to find out anything more that I want to know about. Alf's big brother is already on it, and Alf says it really is fantastic what you can do. There are lots of things on it which are really only meant for grown-ups. But it's only the really clever grown-ups, who are really good at computers, who know how to shut things out that we're not supposed to see; like they think they've done on all the ones we use at school.

The End ..?

Author's final comment:

"This amateur club actually did exist, back in the 1980's and from time to time in various forms, it held similar meetings on many occasions. I'm sure the tradition is being carried on nowadays via the many Chat Sessions and Message Subject pages you can find on the Internet ... in between all the silly stuff of course."

About the author

Tony Thorne MBE is an Englishman, born and technically educated in London, England, but now living in Austria. He originally qualified as a Chartered Design Engineer and subsequently created a well-known company specializing in Very High temperature processing systems and Cryogenic Medical products.

For developments in the field of low temperature (cryo)surgery instruments, the Queen awarded him an MBE. Later he created, and became CEO of, the European Division of an American Corporation specialising in medical laboratory, and computer-related, products.

He has written papers and articles for several technical publications, and has held patents, in such varied fields as nuclear protection clothing, very high temperature furnaces and microbiological laboratory equipment. He also wrote and published his popular semi-autobiography, How to be a Top Executive.

Now retired, he has become an author of short story collections, several non-fiction books, and three novels. He has publishers in America, England, and China. His website URL is: ww.tonythornembe.com

The Author's other publications include…

TENERIFE – Tall Tales with a Twist (Whortleberry Press, USA), The POINTS OF VIEW trilogy (Eternal Press/Caliburn Press, USA), FUTURE REASSURED, FUTURE UNCERTAIN, ROBOTS INCLUDED, TALL SF TALES FOR TEENAGERS, MORE TALL TENERIFE TALES, EVEN MORE TENERIFE TALES, MACABRE

TALES, THREE CULTURE SHOCKS, TIME TRAVEL TROUBLE, THE SINGULARITY IS COMING, (Etcetera Press)

Satire - HOW TO BE A TOP EXECUTIVE, THE QUALITY OF LIFE, THE JUNIOR PHILOSOPHICAL SOCIETY, INSIDE INFORMATION (Etcetera Press Publications)

Poetry - SECOND OPINION [The Poets Yearbook], SHOWCASE – The Guernsey Poets (Editor/contributor), and the websites AUTHOR"S DEN, SCIFINITY, and ABANDONED TOWERS MAGAZINE.

Plus Stories, Poems & Articles in various magazines, anthologies and websites, including PLANET, NEBULA, BSFM, CATS AROUND THE CHRISTMAS TREE and SANTA'S GIVINGS & MISGIVINGS, STRANGE MYSTERIES etc. (5 Whortleberry Press Anthologies); CREATURES OF GLASS & LIGHT (The EuroCon2007 anthology), AXXON (Argentina Magazine), SPICK, ORBIT, ART & PROSE, ALIEN SKIN MAGAZINE, ASTONISHING STORIES, plus NO HORNS ON THESE HELMETS (Anthology).

www.tonythornembe.com

Etcetera Press

16487394R00068

Printed in Great Britain
by Amazon